The Little

HANDBOOK

to Perfecting the

Art of Christian Writing

The Little

HANDBOOK

to Perfecting the

Art of Christian Writing

Getting Your Foot in the Publisher's Door

Leonard G. Goss & Don M. Aycock

BROADMAN
&HOLMAN
PUBLISHERS

Nashville, Tennessee

Ten-digit ISBN:0-8054-3264-7
Thirteen-digit ISBN: 0-8054-3264-0

Published by Broadman & Holman Publishers
Nashville, Tennessee

Dewey Decimal Classification: 808
Subject Heading: CHRISTIAN LITERATURE—
TECHINIQUE \ AUTHORSHIP \ CREATIVE WRITING

2 3 4 5 6 7 8   10 09 08 07 06

I dedicate this book to Joseph and David, my beloved sons, to Carol and Lori, my daughters-in-love, and to Lia Fei and Madeline Marie, my lovely granddaughters.

—Leonard G. Goss

I dedicate this work to Carla, my wife, who has coaxed words from me I didn't even know existed.

—Don M. Aycock

Acknowledgments

When you begin reading this book, you will quickly discover that although two names are on the cover as authors, many people had their hands and minds involved in making this book. We especially thank the following people for their contributions:

Sally Stuart for providing the foreword and for her decades of helping us fellow writers at least act like we know what we're supposed to be doing.

The following writers, editors, agents, and conference directors for their candor and useful perspectives on the publishing business: Ted Baehr, Vicki Caruana, Stephen Clark, Jan Coleman, Reg Forder, Janet Kobobel Grant, Ted Griffin, Lin Johnson, Deidre Knight, Steve Laube, Andy LePeau, Chip MacGregor, Kathi Macias, Alan Maki, Cec Murphey, Marvin Olasky, Susan Titus Osborn, Sally Stuart, Gary Terashita, Ken Walker, and Terry Whalin. We thank them for the permission to use their insights.

The entire staff at Broadman & Holman Publishers, including Steve Bond, David Chandler, Diana Lawrence, Kim Overcash, Dean Richardson, David Shepherd, and Ken Stephens have made this project both fun and, we hope, valuable to the writing community. Our wives, Carolyn and Carla, have given us unwavering encouragement while putting up with the frequent and prolonged physical and mental absences. Without them this book would not have materialized, and we owe them big time.

Contents

Foreword

I hear from writers almost every day who have a burning desire to write, have been writing for years and didn't know what to do with it, or feel God has called them to write their own unique story. The one overarching concern most of them bring to me is the sense that they don't know where to start or how to approach what they see as a daunting task. The world of book publishing seems foreign and overwhelming—fraught with unforeseen pitfalls. In some ways they are not far wrong, but here is a book that is not only going to take them step-by-step through those shaky first steps toward publication, but will give them firm footing as they learn each step to follow along the way.

Don Aycock and Len Goss have already earned a reputation for doing books that help writers on their journey toward publication. Their own extensive experience in the publishing industry has prepared them to develop books that are both practical and filled with all the pertinent information a writer needs to do their job better and more efficiently.

Besides being filled with practical advice and an inside look at the workings of Christian publishing, this book will also inspire you to look more closely at your reasons for writing and inspire you to not only launch into this writing world, but will also help you find the motivation to complete the task.

The decision to actually write a book is a personal one that involves a great deal of prayerful introspection. This book will guide you through that process and also help you determine whether you are undertaking this project to bring help and hope to your reader or just to meet your own needs. Goss's and Aycock's own commitment to honesty in shedding light on this path to publication will help you honestly evaluate your own motives. Their honest assessment of your challenges as a writer will take you from dream to solid reality in a few well-placed steps.

Once you have determined you are going to undertake a book, the important thing will be understanding how to prepare, where to start, and how to keep the process moving ahead. Getting a book published these days is as much about an inside understanding of the industry as it is about the actual writing.

One of the real values of this book for the Christian is that it is written specifically for writers who want to write for the Christian market, giving you valuable insights into both how that market functions and how you can function within it. The authors' long experience and inside knowledge of its inner workings will put you ahead of the competition. They also draw on the knowledge and experiences of other successful Christian writers to help you recognize and tackle the challenges that lie ahead for you as a writer. Instead of decreeing that there is only one way to approach a book project, the shared experiences of those working writers shows you there are many ways to accomplish the task.

Now when I hear from those frustrated writers who don't know where to go from here, I will refer them to this little treasure of inspiration, how-to, and inside information to get them started on their way to a published book that will bless and enrich the lives of their readers.

—Sally E. Stuart
Christian Writers' Market Guide
www.stuartmarket.com

Write in a Book What You See

> Take up our quarrel with the foe.
> To you from failing hands we throw
> The torch, be yours to hold it high.
> —John McCrae, "In Flanders Fields"

Do you remember how the movie *The Sound of Music* begins? It starts way up in the heavens. At first you are so high you see nothing, and you hear only the rush of wind. You are lost in the magnificence of God's creation. Then from this loftiest and highest of vantage points, the camera begins to sweep quickly downward at a dizzying speed. There is a grand camera sweep that goes down farther and farther, down through the clouds, out of the heavens and onto the Earth, until suddenly you are on a mountaintop as the camera focuses on Maria Von Trapp. She begins singing her heart out. The hills are alive with the sound of music! She dances and leaps for joy in God's creation, and we are there with her, having been carried by the camera from the heights of the heavens down to the sunny Austrian mountaintop, and then down to the young girl, Maria.

Do you know that the Gospel of John does something of the same thing? The apostle John begins on a cosmic level: "In the beginning was the Word, and the Word was with God, and the Word was God" (John 1:1). Then John begins a grand camera sweep, moving from the Creator down to the creation, for "the Word became flesh and took up residence among us. We observed His glory, the glory as the One and Only Son from the Father, full of grace and truth." The Word was made flesh through the Incarnation. God was there first, with the first word. He spoke creation into existence. This is the first demonstration we have that words are powerful. Creation and salvation came through words.

Bearing the Human Soul

Words have power and importance not only in the heavenlies. The camera is still sweeping downward when the Gospel writer tells us, "There was a man named John who was sent from God" (John 1:6). This other John, John the Baptist, used words, too, to witness to the Light. He cried out, "This was the One of whom I said, 'The One coming after me has surpassed me, because He existed before me'" (v. 15). Words are the vehicles of God's truth. Because of the power of words, the magnificence of God was revealed through John the Baptist.

Could the words we write be powerful and significant, such that the magnificence of God could be revealed through them? The coauthors suggest they can. As many others have pointed out, all the great movements of human history came about through the activities of writing and publishing. Think of Israel's remarkable reformation under Josiah when the Book of the Law was discovered after being abandoned in the temple. Remember the Jews who were permitted to return to Jerusalem to rebuild their temple when Cyrus king of Persia put a proclamation in writing. Think of the four Gospel narratives that energized the life of the early Christian church. Or think of the sixteenth-century Protestant Reformation, when Martin Luther's writings circulated in Europe. In ancient as well as modern times, the great intellectual paradigm shifts have come from writing and publishing.

In her book *Sword Blades and Poppy Seed,* Amy Lowell said, "All books are either dreams or swords." The cataclysmic movements of history were led by vibrant dreams, and today the word-processing keyboard can be an effective and sharp sword. What is the point? It is that what we write and publish can in a realistic way transform our readers' lives.

A woman telephoned the Atlanta library and asked where Scarlett O'Hara was buried. The librarian told the woman that Scarlett O'Hara is a fictional character out of Margaret Mitchell's story *Gone with the Wind.* After hearing this, the caller then said, "Never mind that. I want to know where she's buried." For the caller Scarlett O'Hara was made alive in that novel! Good books live, and they move people, for what happens in the mind of someone who reads a good book can be absolutely dynamic. Emily Dickinson hardly ever left her home, yet she went on many travels through her reading. She wrote:

> There is no Frigate like a book
> To take us Lands away
> Nor any Coursers like a Page

Of Prancing Poetry.
This traverse may the poorest take
Without oppress of Toll—
How Frugal is the Chariot
That bears the Human Soul.

Let us ask our readers a question. Do you want to write nonfiction books, novels, articles, drama, screenplays, and poetry that bare the human soul? Are you interested in writing that reveals the heart and core of the story of God? That would be an immense challenge, worthy of our highest talents. Are you called to do it? One day while serving his prison term on the island of Patmos, the apostle John was called to write. He was in the Spirit on the Lord's Day when he heard a voice like a trumpet say, "Write in a book what you see, and send it to the seven churches" (Rev. 1:11 NASB). The originator of that call was none other than God's Spirit.

Sowing Tears

Has that call come to you? If and when it does, it will come in an unequivocal and unedited form—and have no doubt, it will come from God's Spirit. And when it does come, you should be ready and prepared. Motivation and desire are not enough. You don't need genius, but you do need deep preparation and a complete set of tools, including market books and magazines, dictionaries, grammar books, style guides, histories of language, critique groups, writing conferences, library and online computer research techniques, a knowledge of how to get and preserve ideas, a sense of what editors need and how to approach them, all the how-to advice you can collect, and an instinctive grasp of grammar, syntax, and words.

If you don't love words, please don't bother thinking about writing. It will be more work than you will ever want to do. Don't be lazy like Huckleberry Finn. Huck closed his story with these words: "There ain't nothing more to write about, and I am rotten glad of it, because if I'd a' knowed what a trouble it was to make a book I wouldn't a' tackled it, and ain't a-going to no more." Huck Finn might have been lazy, but Mark Twain wasn't. If you want the fruit, climb the tree. As Shakespeare said in *King Lear,* "Nothing will come of nothing." In Psalm 126:5, King David said it this way: "Those who sow in tears will reap with shouts of joy." You will have to sow some tears to write in a way that bares the human soul.

Are you ready to sow some tears? The number of Christians who are ready is almost amazing, and the number seems to be increasing. In a way this should not be surprising. God has given us the gift of books. We write them and publish them to please ourselves and others who, like us, love and want books. And we publish them because people depend on books to build a strong foundation. Books have the depth to let thinkers develop their thoughts and engage in dialogue with others. They enable one generation to leave a heritage for the next. In short, the world needs the value of books, and people who write them enjoy their association with books and ideas and with people who love books and ideas. For the bibliophile books are not luxuries but absolute necessities.

Discovering What This Life Is For

God has given us the gift of words. At their best, words are windows into the soul of another person—the writer.

Perhaps this is why the printed word holds such a permanent place in the ranks of human achievement. What do these windows to the soul admit? Among other things, knowledge, inspiration, challenge, motivation, hope, and plain fun to millions who read and to a smaller number who write. Do you doubt it? Visit a bookstore and watch the ravenous looks in the patrons' eyes as they relish each title and devour each cover.

Saul Bellow has written that there is "an immense, painful longing for a broader, more flexible, fuller, more coherent, more comprehensive account of what we human beings are, who we are, and what this life is for." *That* is why we write and publish—to help readers discover what this life is for. The real business of Christian writing and publishing is promoting ideas. It is no exaggeration to say that we hold in our hands the power to mold minds, and we work in this field with a deep sense of responsibility. We try to offer answers to readers through writing and publishing in the same way the Gospels tell us Jesus offered answers to his hearers on the vital religious, political, and social issues of his day—by mooring them in stories of personal accountability. Through stories the entire Bible conveys the good news that God has entered into the story of his creation. Our challenge as Christian writers and publishers is to pursue excellence in promoting that story.

Six Steps to Get Ready

What should you do to prepare to promote that story? First, wait on God and depend on him. David wrote, "Be still before the LORD and wait patiently for him; do not fret" (Ps. 37:7 NIV). Learn to put your writing project on the shelf for a time if that seems necessary—especially when it is giving you fits and there is no joy in it anymore. Put it aside, and wait until God wants you to go back to it. Learn to expect God to help you. Like David, we should learn to say, "But I will hope continually and will praise You more and more. . . . I will proclaim Your righteousness, Yours alone" (Ps. 71:14, 16).

Second, put on your armor and take a stand. Paul wrote, "Put on the full armor of God so that you can take your stand against the devil's schemes. For our struggle is not against flesh and blood, but against the rulers, against the authorities, against the powers of this dark world and against the spiritual forces of evil in the heavenly realms. Therefore put on the full armor of God" (Eph. 6:11–13 NIV).

Third, during battle keep your eyes on the Leader. "Fix your eyes on Jesus, the author and perfecter of our faith," as the writer of Hebrews tells us, "who for the joy that lay before Him endured a cross and despised the shame, and has sat down at the right hand of God's throne" (Heb. 12:2).

Fourth, pursue excellence. Why shouldn't what we write be absolutely excellent and the best it can be in every way? We have the world's best message of hope. Shouldn't that bring out the best writing in us? Ecclesiastes 9:10a says, "Whatever your hands find to do, do with [all] your strengths. . . ."

Fifth, uncover the truth wherever it can be found. This requires wide reading if you are going to be an excellent writer. On occasion this may even require reading things that go against the aesthetic and moral grain of our beliefs. Remember that St. Augustine used the popular songs of his day to attack heretics. John Calvin and Martin Luther did the same thing, putting Christian lyrics to popular melodies. Before he became a Christian, St. Augustine read the books of the Platonists translated from Greek into Latin. After he became a Christian, he wrote, "From the Gentiles indeed I had come to know You; and I fixed my mind upon the gold which You will that Your people should bring with them from Egypt: for it was Yours, wherever it was." John Calvin said this of some of the secular writers he read: "We cannot read them without great admiration. We marvel at them because we are compelled to recognize how preeminent they are. . . . Those men whom Scripture call 'natural men' were indeed sharp and penetrating in their investigations of interior things. Let us accordingly learn from their example how many gifts the Lord left to human nature. . . . If the Lord has willed that we be helped . . . let us use this assistance." What matters is truth. If truth is being preached by secular writers, then so be it. The truth is one truth wherever it is found, and all truth is God's truth. Paul said that "we demolish arguments and every high-minded thing that is raised up against the knowledge of God, taking every thought captive to the obedience of Christ" (2 Cor. 10:5).

Sixth, proclaim freedom. You don't have to stick to any one form or kind of writing. Be versatile. The Oxford professor Charles Lutwidge Dodgson wrote mathematics textbooks, but he also put on another hat and took another name—Lewis Carroll—when he wrote about Alice's adventures in Wonderland. Be free, indeed, and proclaim freedom in your writing. Proclaiming freedom also means writing as a free person, proclaiming freedom for prisoners and recovery of sight for the blind. As John said, "If the Son sets you free, you will be free indeed" (John 8:36 NIV). In his own hometown synagogue, Jesus said, "The Spirit of the Lord is on me, because he has anointed me to preach good news . . . He has sent me to proclaim freedom" (Luke 4:18 NIV). As writers we should live as free men and women, not as though our freedom was there to provide a screen for wrongdoing or a way to conceal evil but rather as slaves in God's service, as Peter said in 1 Peter 2:16. Martin Luther put it this way: "A Christian man is the most free lord of all, and subject to none; a Christian man is the most dutiful servant of all, and subject to everyone."

Our whole purpose in writing this book is to share our excitement regarding Christian writing on an intimate, personal basis. We have picked up tips, pointers, no-no's, maybes, and musts about writing along the way. We want to make these available to you. There is no *one* way to do it, but there are some generally accepted principles and methods of going about the writing of books and getting those books published. If we can help you, our readers, make even a single step toward getting ready to write and publish, then our purpose will be served.

When you're ready, remember that the Lord is sending you to release the oppressed and to proclaim the year of the Lord's favor. That is a great work and a high calling. Do it the best and truest way you know. Then write in a book what you see.

CHAPTER 1
What You Ought to Know about Christian Writing and Publishing

Books have been used as God's tools throughout the history of the church, and writing and publishing continue to fill a unique place in the church's work in the modern world. When you consider that writers and editors make crucial decisions about what people in all phases of church life will read, you will realize that books are strategic in helping Christians be salt and light in society.

Words are a divine gift and powerful tools in the hands of good writers and editors. We have also been given the gifts of books and writing, which allow us to share our hopes and dreams as well as our disappointments and sorrows. Along with the incarnation of Christ and next to oral preaching and teaching, God has chosen the medium of books to proclaim his Kingdom. Put another way, God's Word is spoken to be heard, but it is also written and printed to be read. Books are much more than mere commodities—products with covers, pages with ink on them, and bindings. Books actually can change lives, and many have throughout history. In his *Sesame and Lilies,* John Ruskin said, "All books are divisible into two classes: the books of the hour, and the books of all time." Think of it. The books you write possibly could be books for all time or at least books that effectively communicate truth in our own time.

A Bleak Future?

The real business of Christian writing and publishing, then, is not only selling books, as important as that is. The real business is promoting ideas—the ideas of the Kingdom. The real business of Christian writing and publishing makes a difference in the unseen world as well as in the seen world.

Now admittedly, all of this is theoretical. On the more practical level, what sort of opportunity do we *really* face as writers and publishers? Is writing and publishing in the Christian arena worth our time and effort? Consider these facts.

Roughly one-half of all Americans read only *one* book each year. The pool of illiterates in the United States is growing by about 2.3 million people yearly. This includes school dropouts, immigrants, and refugees. But the problem is not just *illiteracy*; it is also *aliteracy*. Many people actually are not illiterate, yet they are such poor readers that they cannot draw simple inferences from written material. And they could never write a persuasive essay. Then there are some people who can read, but they just *don't,* except under compulsion. They read enough barely to get by.

There used to be a pet rock craze in this country. Maybe pet rocks are not as popular now, but it is possible there are more people willing to buy a pet rock than a book. Most people think that rocks are at least real, but ideas—the sorts of ideas one finds in books—are not real (even though many more people have been killed by ideas than by rocks). Ideas are very real, but to get at ideas requires reading, and this is something fewer and fewer people are either able or willing to do. Not many of us readers are left. So the fact that many people just do not read is one problem. If this is true, does this mean that the book will soon be dead?

The new electronic publishing technology is another problem. Hasn't it almost killed the need to write and publish books? Enthusiasts for the new technology have in fact been predicting the demise of the book for many years. For one thing, think about the cost of paper, which has risen at an incredible rate, along with the amount of human energy needed to move it and the volume of space required to store it. Does this suggest a more efficient method of conveying information than in the typical printed book? Some think it does and that that method is electronic. Does the ascendancy of the computer and electronic books mean we should be writing an obituary for the poor and lowly book? If so, why should anyone be concerned with writing and print publishing?

A third reason we might question the need to write and publish is our culture. We live in what nearly everyone is calling a post-Christian climate. Because of the utter contempt the wider culture has not only for Christianity and objective truth generally but also for the old-world print culture, we will continue to write and publish books and articles for a smaller and smaller subculture. How can we be literary salt and light in a culture that does not accept truth and beauty and aesthetics—in short, in a culture that does not accept us?

Another reason to wonder if we are spending our time wisely and well when working on book manuscripts is that in publishing, even in Christian publishing, our sense of business may be taking over our sense of critical judgment. In other words, the comfort level of those in publishing toward what is being published may be changing. Many in Christian publishing today seem unconcerned abut the *right* choice of what to publish. Rather, they are concerned only with *sales* and bringing their wares to the market. This is the jackpot syndrome. When George Bernard Shaw once said of publishing that "there is probably no other trade in which there is so little relationship between profits and actual value, or into which sheer chance so largely enters," he was describing much of Christian book publishing at the beginning of the twenty-first century. Now the idea is to package books so they appeal only to the general reader representing the blasé Christian mainstream. It is to publish more books that sell in large quantities and fewer books that serve a limited reading audience. It is to compete with the electronic media for the entertainment dollar, to bring all the glitz and visual appeal to books one associates with the electronic media.

Some Christian book publishers have become virtually a subset of the electronic media, and some are owned by conglomerate media companies. With the media takeover of major parts of books publishing, the distribution of books is increasingly in the hands of fewer and fewer people, and the battle is to push the product out the door and to get the books on the bookstore shelves. The main thing is to convince bookstores to stock only those popular titles by well-known authors that are guaranteed to sell quickly. Many of these books are worthwhile, but many of them do little more than mimic the popular culture and popular values. They tend toward sentimentality, celebrity worship, sensationalism, simplistic answers, and self-centered desires. But they sell.

But here is the problem: As Christians, we are supposed to be *in* the world. Who ever said we were supposed to be *of* the world (John 17:14–18)?

Because of the aggressive attempts on the part of some publishing houses to grow the market and because it seems like some would do almost anything to get an overload of product out into the marketplace, some damage is being done to Christian writing and publishing. The reason for this is clear. With this aggressive attempt to grow the market has come an expanding range of what is acceptable material. In order to reach the wider market, now sometimes *anything* is acceptable. One wonders if there is any longer a commitment to high quality writing and publishing, let alone a commitment to any form of serious Christian thinking. In short, what has been affected is the content of what we do.

It is a sad state of affairs when it is not only the post-Christian culture that has contempt for the serious print culture but when some Christian publishers themselves have the same contempt when they will not publish serious books that demand thinking on the part of readers. Don't get us wrong. There is nothing wrong with making money, but when a publishing house exists for one reason and one reason only—to make money for their owners—and when they do this by exploiting trends and publishing fads, then this is a grim time to be involved in Christian writing and publishing. (This is of course also true for those writing in the general reading market.) If we as writers, editors, and publishers marry the spirit of the age, we may soon become widows and widowers.

How many are interested anymore in publishing books of intrinsic excellence? If it is true that we write and print books in an era when the relevance of good books seems to be dying, are we as writers and publishers ourselves responsible for the dying relevance of books? Have we lost our specific calling? Have we no longer any vision? Where is our discernment?

Striking a Blow for the Kingdom

For these reasons and others, the future for writers and publishers may look bleak. Is all lost? The answer is no, all is not lost.

Gene Edward Veith ends his book, *Reading Between the Lines,* by talking about what happened fifteen hundred years ago during the first Dark Age, when the Vandals trashed a civilization based on law and learning. He writes:

> Amidst the moral anarchy, staggering ignorance, and image-centered paganism that prevailed for centuries, the tradition of literacy was preserved in the church. Behind the protective walls of the monasteries, books were cherished. They were copied out by hand, carefully stored, and eagerly read. The church was concerned for all kinds of books—Bibles, of course, but also books of medicine and science, works of pagan philosophers such as Aristotle, the poetry of Virgil and the comedies of Plautus. The Vandal aesthetic may be coming back in the anti-intellectualism of the mass culture and in the Postmodern nihilism of the high culture. Christians may be the last readers. If so, they need to be in training.[1]

The authors believe that, should the Lord tarry, Christian writing and publishing will be here for a long time. In his book *Sixpence House,* author Paul Collins says, "If you grew up in a rural area, you have seen how farmhouses come and go, but the dent left by cellars is permanent. There is something unbreakable in that hand-dug foundational gouge into the earth. Books are the cellars of civilization: when cultures crumble away, their books remain out of sheer stupid solidity. We see their accumulated pages, and marvel— what readers they were!"[2] Let us give you four reasons our books are in no danger of being removed from the scene and why they will make a permanent dent.

First, given their price, books are the most versatile and user-friendly communications packages in existence. One can move from front to back or from back to front, or one can dive into a book at any place. You can go at any speed and snuggle up to a book in front of a fire, or in bed, or take it to the beach or on a vacation to the mountains. Here is the point: Books are tactile in a way that a computer is not. We were told that binding pages together to make books and magazines was going out of fashion when the personal computer was developed. But publishing has been alive since Johann Gutenberg invented typographic printing in the 1400s, and we think we will be making books for a long while to come.

Second, our education will continue to be built around books. The structure of our national life will continue to rest on our books of law, history, politics, religion, geography, art, and biography. Books will continue to be the main source of our reservoir of knowledge about faith, memory, wisdom, morality, poetry, philosophy, history, and science. Daniel Boorstin has said in *The Discoverers* that our civilization is a product of the Culture of the Book. He means that books in their traditional form will continue to encompass us in thousands of ways. People are still motivated by ideas, and books are the principle means by which ideas are given currency and made effective.

According to Barbara Tuchman, "Books are carriers of civilization. Without books, history is silent, literature is dumb, science crippled, thought and speculation at a standstill. Without books, the development of civilization would have been impossible. They are the engines of change, windows on the world, and lighthouses erected in the sea of time. They are companions, teachers, magicians, bankers of the treasure of the mind. Books are humanity in print."

Third, Christian writing and publishing will be here for a long time because God wants and uses them. Put another way, the welfare of the Christian church is tied to the welfare of books and reading. There is a line that goes like this: "Without books God would be silent." Now that is only partially true. If no books were ever published from now on, God would still speak. He spoke through the prophets and through his Son before books as we know them came into being. But God also *does* speak through books.

After all, Christianity actually is called the "religion of the Book." The word *Bible* itself comes from the Greek word that literally means "the book." The welfare of the church is tied closely to the welfare of books because God has chosen books to reveal himself to us. Books have been God's tools throughout history, and many of them have changed history itself. Think of the writings of Martin Luther, Philip Spener, John Wesley, Hannah More, John Newton, and many others.

Books still have something to do with spiritual values and spiritual growth, and this is especially true when publishers continue publishing serious books that veer off radically from the culture and make a real difference in people's lives. If we do that, then certainly the welfare of books will have a lot to do with the fate of Christianity. Some seven hundred years ago, Thomas á Kempis said, "If he shall not lose his reward who gives a cup of cold water to his thirsty neighbor, what will be the reward of those who by putting good books into the hands of those neighbors, open to them the fountain of eternal life?"

A fourth reason for thinking that writing and publishing of a particularly Christian nature will be here for a long time to come is that Christians have to read. We are the people of the Book. Our spirituality is centered upon linguistic revelation. In other words, we believe that books, especially Christian ones, will remain with us because many people, like us, want and need them. Why? Because they do things to us.

Wrestling with Angels

Not all books do things for us, of course. Only the best books do things in a powerful way to readers. It is certainly true that much of what we write and publish is read today and discarded tomorrow, making it irrelevant. It is irrelevant in the sense that it is not unique or compelling, and it does not provide a fresh and distinctively Christian examination of questions confronting people in their personal lives or in the wider culture. Just look at many of the books one can find in an average bookstore. What is there to stimulate us and challenge us that right is better than wrong, that joy is better than grief, and that courage and faith are better than fear and doubt? How many books in a typical Christian bookstore are written by authors of fertile powers, with a full range of imagination? We think there are few. The reason is that we do not develop and publish the best writers in our community, and we do not require the best from the authors we do publish. The result is that many of the books we produce are, in fact, irrelevant.

Think of the field of fiction. In the typical Christian bookstore, where would you turn to find an authentic novel of religious experience that is as good as Henry Roth's *Call It Sleep,* a story of the Jewish experience? Where would you find a book on the struggle toward religious certainty that is as good as T. S. Eliot's *Ash Wednesday*? Could you locate an allegorical novel on the basic human condition that was as brilliant as Katherine Anne Porter's *Ship of Fools*? What real-life story has come out of the Christian writing community that is as prescient an account of the human condition as Richard Wright's *Black Boy*? If you wanted to recommend a novel that delves into doubt and the sinful human condition of despair, what novel could you recommend in a Christian bookstore that would even begin to compare with Herman Melville's *Moby Dick*? These books were written by relentlessly equipped writers. How many of such writers have appeared from the Christian community? The writers of these books may not have been writing about the Bible, but in their writing they looked into the landscape of the Bible and brought out the indomitable words in the Bible. Really great fiction is literature of power. In A *Christmas Carol,* Charles Dickens shows that generosity is better than miserliness. Fyodor Dostoevsky's *The Brothers Karamazov* shows how Christ brings meaning into a meaningless world. Great writing fills an abyss. It stands beyond, behind, and within the passing flux of immediate things. But much of what we as writers, editors, and publishers do is trivial, and it will not last.

Lest we be too negative, we should not forget that if we do our writing the best we can, using all the gifts and talents God has given us, there is every chance it can move and change people, doing things to them in powerful ways. Far from being irrelevant, our books can be literature of power, books that are radical in our time and do much to change the world—as previous books were radical in their times and did much to change their worlds. They can motivate readers, much as, for example, Harriet Beecher Stowe's *Uncle Tom's Cabin* or Alexander Solzhenitsyn's *The Gulag Archipelago* did.

Writing is a challenge and a process, and to develop diligence and skill is hard work. Writing is frustrating. It is like Jacob wrestling with the angel; all you can do is hold on for as long as you can until someone calls your name—until you find just the right word or line or expression. If you are earnest about the writing art, you need to pay in serious work and preparation. There is no room for less than that.

Notes

1. Gene Edward Veith, *Reading Between the Lines* (Wheaton, Ill.: Crossway Books, 1990).

2. Paul Collins, *Sixpence House* (New York: Bloomsbury, 2003).

CHAPTER 2
Writing: The Truth and Nothing but the Truth

I am always interested in why young people become writers, and from talking with many I have concluded that most do not want to be writers working eight and ten hours a day and accomplishing little; they want to have been writers, garnering the rewards of having completed a best-seller. They aspire to the rewards of writing but not to the travail.

—James A. Michener

The music business is a cruel and shallow money trench, a long plastic hallway where thieves and pimps run free, and good men die like dogs. There's also a negative side.

—Hunter S. Thompson

Congratulations?

Sorry to start off on such a downer with these two quotes, but we vowed to be honest in this book. Michener is right in realizing that many writers want the rewards but not the labor of the writing life. And Thompson, while characterizing the music rather than the publishing business, is on target about people's perceptions about the business side of the creative life. It can be bloody.

But here you are anyway—you wish to write a book. We're not entirely sure whether to offer congratulations or condolences. Estimates are that should your book be published, it will compete against 150,000 titles and new editions published in the same year. Think of it! And that is just from the commercial publishers. Today, many smaller, print-on-demand presses whip out books in as little as four weeks. They may add another forty thousand titles. Your competition may be somewhere close to 200,000 titles! Imagine how many manuscripts are submitted to publishers that never see the light of day. It boggles the mind.

But we writers are a strange breed. You are thinking, *Yeah, I know the competition is stiff, but mine won't be one of the rejected manuscripts. Surely mine will make it.* We applaud your courage and tenacity. We have put this book together to help you realize that dream of seeing your book in print.

The Authors' Assumptions

We assume several things about you, the reader of this book. We assume first that you have something vital you want to say in the book you contemplate writing. Because yours is a religious book (or else why would you be reading this guide?), it can help people live more fulfilled, complete lives. Not long ago religious books were seen as "fluff books"—usually dramatic conversions, celebrities' accounts of their "faith," or oversimplified approaches to difficult problems. There are still many of these "difficult-problem/easy-answers" books out there, but overall the quality of all Christian writing is getting better. Put another way, some of the books that were published even a decade ago would probably not get produced today. The bar is higher than at any time since Gutenberg invented movable type.

Do not get us wrong. We are not against all stories of celebrity conversions and advice based on experience. It is just that the reading public's tastes are changing. They are demanding the cookies be put on higher shelves, in high-quality books with more sound themes to help readers think through issues and find real solutions. They want material with more substance and less fluff. You can deliver such books to publishers ready to develop, produce, and market them. The next section of this chapter expands this idea a little more.

A second assumption about you is that you want to share your vital message in written form. You are willing to spend the hours of seemingly endless toil necessary for good writing. You are willing to give up watching your favorite television show, including Sunday afternoon football games, and put up with comments from family and friends like, "Aw, she's *only* writing a book." We devote little space in this guide trying to pique your interest in writing. If you lack interest, then do not waste your time reading this book for inspiration.

Our third idea about you is that you know the rudiments of English grammar, spelling, syntax, and all the other bits and pieces of information your high school English teacher kept saying you would need to know someday. That someday is now. If you need to refresh yourself, as we all occasionally do, go to a local library or bookstore and read one or two good primers on grammar. Many Web sites can help you with these rudiments of producing readable manuscripts. Writing styles are as individual as fingerprints, but certain guidelines do exist. You need to know the basic principles.

What about Religious Books?

The tastes and demands of a reading public change. At one time, books on religious themes were looked at with suspicion, both by many readers and by the publishing industry. More than one person suggested that subsidy publishers (or vanity presses—you pay them to publish your book) made money on books with religious subjects because so few in publishing would touch them. Referring to this type of publisher, one observer noted, "They offer a bland, steady flow of essays that God is love, nature is true, and in the long run, the Spirit triumphs."

Have things changed today! Just look at the success of books like the Left Behind series by Tim LaHaye and Jerry Jenkins. Today, even major secular publishers are pushing hard to add religious topics to their lineup. Some publishers have either started their own religious imprint line or bought an established religious publishing house. They have discovered something many of us have known for a long time—people are hungry for high-quality, spiritually uplifting books and articles.

Today, many religious books outsell nonreligious titles. We are not referring to the poorly written banal tomes in which some subsidy publishers specialize. Well-written books with vital themes in religion have proved they have a place in the publishing world. Rick Warren's book *The Purpose-Driven Life* has surpassed the twenty-million-sales mark! Dozens of highly professional firms specialize in publishing religious titles. A major company that specializes in women's magazines and craft books recently started a religious publishing line. They found that inspirational books made up the fastest-growing segment of publishing. Because of this fact, they signed several well-known authors to initiate their line of books.

Writing: The Beginning

You have a great idea for an article or book. But you are asking yourself, "How do I get started?" and "Am I really sure I can do this?" Almost all writers ask these questions, so you are in good company.

Remember that language—the coinage of our work—is a living entity. It changes and grows. Everyone who has struggled to learn a foreign language knows this reality. Language can even be invented. Mark Okrand created a language for the popular Star Trek series and movies—Klingon. He also created Vulcan for Mr. Spock and others. Okrand came up with the idea for Atlantean in the movie, *Atlantis—the Lost Empire.* So much interest followed the Klingon phenomenon that Okrand wrote a dictionary for the newly invented language. In an interview with Lucia Anderson, he claims that there are hundreds of Klingon speakers in forty-five countries.

J. R. R. Tolkien invented languages for his Lord of the Rings trilogy too. These languages—Sindarin and Queen, the Elvish tongues and Dwarvish—took on a life of their own when the books were made into movies. David Salo was working on a PhD degree in linguistics when he was asked to help invent dialogue using these made-up languages. A line of dialogue between Aragorn and Arwen goes like this:

"Renich i l i erui govannem?" "Nauthannen i ned l reniannen."

Salo is so proficient at these languages now he can point out where Tolkien made mistakes writing it out! In an interview with Susan Lambert Smith, Salo says, "Just because you invented the language doesn't mean you're the best at writing it out."

Yes, language is a living, changing medium of communication. Poet Robert Frost spoke of his craft in nuptial terms. He said the poet marries the language, and out of that union the poem is born. As you learn to write for publication, you will be learning to love language with all of its subtleties, difficulties, and grandeurs. It will become your servant as you use it to shape your thoughts. It will clothe your imagination and give your senses free reign to explore the full scope of human life and redemption in Jesus Christ.

Getting It Done

Let us consider the counsel of several well-known and highly respected authors of religious books. If we learn from their experiences, we might be able to avoid some of the traps and pitfalls most writers face. There are obviously other writers than these listed here, but these have been chosen because of their impact, as well as the fact that their work has stood the test of time.

William Barclay

One of the best-known religious authors of our time was the late William Barclay, a Scottish professor of divinity. Barclay wrote scores of important books during his career as teacher and writer. His books have sold into the millions, and they are still selling well among pastors and divinity students all over the world.

Barclay's philosophy of writing was deceptively obvious. He said, "I can and do work." In other words, he was willing to pay the price for writing. He quoted Collin Brooks, who defined this process as follows: "The art of writing is the art of applying the seat of the pants to the seat of the chair." And he was not talking about the chair at the dinner table!

Barclay said he was influenced by his fellow British author, Winston Churchill. Churchill was a writer of incredible discipline. His multiple-volume history of the Second World War attests to this fact. At his birthplace outside Oxford, England, Blenheim Palace, Churchill had an elaborate library and study. One can tell immediately that he took his writing seriously.

First-time authors sometimes do not take their writing seriously. But they can be assured that if they do not, no one else will. These writers are tempted to "wait for inspiration" before beginning. Perhaps they have never heard the dictum, "Good writing is 10 percent inspiration and 90 percent perspiration."

Someone once asked Churchill about inspiration, distractions, and other things that thwart an author's effort. His answer was typically pointed and slightly gruff: "You've got to get over that. If you sit waiting for inspiration, you will sit waiting until you are an old man. Writing is like any other job—like marching an army, for instance. If you sit down and wait until the weather is fine, you won't get far with your troops. Kick yourself; irritate yourself; but *write;* it's the only way."

William Barclay learned his lesson well from his mentor. He worked hard at "applying the seat of the pants to the seat of the chair." Barclay's students knew well his work habits. Whenever he was not busy teaching classes or talking with his students about academic matters, he could be found at all times pounding on his typewriter. But, and his former students underscored this point, Barclay *always* had time for his students. As much as he worked at it, writing was not his only way of discipling Christians.

Other than tenacity, Barclay denied having any special gift for writing. In fact, he claimed never to have an original thought in his life. He called himself a "pipeline" or a "theological middleman." He felt he could take the large bills of theology and philosophy and break them down into small change so average persons could understand. Of course, the ability to do this takes uncommon skill and superior talent and intellect. Because he was willing to do so, millions of people have benefited from the labor of William Barclay.

This brings us to a point that must be emphasized and reemphasized: the person who wants to write must work extremely hard. One of the authors once queried an editor about a book he wanted to do. The editor answered immediately and said he was interested. He wanted to see three chapters, but they were not ready. When the author beat around the bush about them, that editor wrote a short, never-to-be-forgotten note. It said, "The only way to learn to write is to write. Well?"

Max Lucado

Barclay represents one way of writing—the lone writer working away in a room. Let us now take a more contemporary writer whose approach is different. Max Lucado is one of the most prolific writers today. He is the longtime pastor at Oak Hill Church in San Antonio, Texas. Lucado has produced more than fifty books that have sold in excess of thirty million copies. Most of his books are expansions of his pulpit ministry. He chooses a topic for study and preaching each year. He will do the background work and then write a sermon manuscript. He gives a copy of that manuscript to his assistant, Karen Hill. She makes notes on the manuscript as Lucado delivers the sermon.

After the sermon, Lucado and Hill work with longtime editor Liz Heaney to produce a book. Lucado does the basic writing using his keen sense of words and images to produce some of the most popular books of the past fifteen years. He is known for using apt metaphors and analogies that help people understand relationships to both God and others. So popular are his words that they have been licensed for DVDs, music, booklets, giftware, study Bibles, and even Hallmark cards.

Lucado speaks of his writing in an interview with Cindy Crosby in *Christianity Today*:

> I don't play much golf. All of my sermons
> become books. That helps. I have a great
> ministerial team. And the elders at the church, all

they want me to do is preach. That's been our arrangement. I preach about forty Sundays a year. I'm gradually working toward maybe thirty-five because we're wanting to train some other young ministers. About four weeks out of the year I just write, and that's in January and February. What I do is I take the sermon series from the year before, and I turn that into a book. If the church needs to hear it, then maybe it will speak to the broader market.

Lucado's writing has given him open doors to many places of influence. David Moberg, senior vice president and publisher for W Publishing Group, says, "Max Lucado is becoming, for many people, America's pastor, much in the tradition of Norman Vincent Peale or Billy Graham. I think that's his future."

Not bad for a guy whose first book was turned down by fourteen publishers.

Jan Karon

Not every author who becomes successful starts off with a bang. Nearly every writer who eventually makes it has had to battle every obstacle imaginable. That is as true of Jan Karon as of anyone else. Karon worked in advertising for many years and was, by her own account, successful. But spiritually she felt unsatisfied. She hungered for meaning. She hungered for God. She says, "I was so starved for God that it was more than I could bear. One night I got on my knees on my bed, and I begged God to save my soul. I asked Jesus to come into my heart."

In Diane Eble's book on writing, *Behind the Stories,* Karon tells how she spent two years in prayer about her future. She eventually quit the advertising business and moved into a small cottage in the mountains near family members. Armed with a used computer, she began writing about people and situations that interested her. No publisher seemed interested in her work. With her income cut in half, Karon went without a car for a year. But she kept writing and pushing ahead. One evening during a time of prayer, she had a vision of a priest walking down a village street. She says, "I decided to submit it to my imagination and see where it went. And then it went to a dog named Barnabas and a boy named Doolie, and the story began to tell itself to me."

This was the beginning of the now-famous Mitford series. The book was first serially published in Karon's local newspaper, *The Blowing Rocket*. Fame and fortune were not instantaneous. She gave the book manuscript to an agent who held it a year and a half without doing much with it. She took it back and began sending it out herself but got rejected time and time again. Eventually a publisher bought it but did little to promote it. But Karon, with an advertising background, took matters into her own hands. She went to book signings and did everything possible to make her work known. After the second book in the series was published, a bookseller suggested to Karon that she talk to a well-known agent in New York. She did and the agent seemed to understand what the books were all about. The agent sent them to Penguin, who really got behind the books with publicity and financial support. Today, more than eight million copies later, Jan Karon's books delight readers worldwide.

It was a tough climb, but Karon realizes every writer will face similar challenges. She says, "There *will* be challenges. I don't care where you are, I don't care how much money you have to tide you over while you're trying to write your book or change careers or whatever, God is going to call us all into a hard place to work for him. God can't give you a gift to touch other people in a variety of ways unless he has put you in the valley in a variety of ways. That's the only way we can ever reach people."

Consensus

When we take the experiences of William Barclay, Max Lucado, Jan Karon, and many other writers, add them together factoring in their advice to new writers, what do we get?

First, if you are serious about writing, you must write. This sounds absurdly obvious, but many people miss it. The only way to get experience is to get experience.

Second, you need a quiet, private place where you can write. Not everyone has the luxury of owning a lavish private office or cabin by the beach. But almost everyone can find some space to call his or her own, at least for an hour or two. Your family will understand and, if requested, learn to leave you alone for awhile.

Third, develop a routine that is right for *you*. You may not even feel awake until noon. If so, then trying to write in the mornings will be frustrating and futile. Find what time of day or night is best for you and work creatively. Line up the tools that best suit your needs. For example, can you write better with a typewriter or a computer, or do you need to write everything in longhand? Perhaps you can do both. Most books on writing suggest the use of a typewriter or computer because it is faster than writing with a pencil.

Fourth, be willing to revise and edit your own work. It can *always* be better. Your words can be expanded, rearranged, or even deleted without the universe suffering irreparable damage. Too many religious writers have the notion that inspired writing is writing *directly* inspired by God and therefore requires no editing. God *does* inspire writers with the divine creative nudge. But this does not negate the necessity to edit and rewrite serious work. If your work actually has been inspired, if you want it to count for something, then you must handle it as a sacred trust and polish it to a fine edge.

Fifth, submit your work to God. He has given you a gift and asks you what you are going to do with it. The only legitimate answer is to use it for his glory.

By now you see how hard writing books can be. At the same time you should also see what joy writing can add to your life.

Writing for Quantity

Let us give you some statistics that might possibly shock you, but we hope they will also inspire you when you think about cranking out a book or two.

Charles Hamilton, alias Frank Richards, creator of "Billy Bunter," averaged writing eighty thousand words a week. This is about 320 pages per week, or sixty-four pages daily.

Georges Simenon, a Belgian writer and creator of "Inspector Maigret," wrote a two-hundred-page novel in eight days. From 1919 to 1973 he wrote 214 novels under his own name and three hundred others under nineteen other pen names. His books, including many translations, sold three hundred million copies.

John Creasey wrote 564 books in his lifetime. Once he wrote two books in six and a half days.

Earle Stanley Gardner had 140 titles of his books published. Over 170 million copies sold.

Ursula Bloom published 468 full-length books from 1922 to 1972. That is an average of more than nine per year.

Walter Gibson, creator of "The Shadow," wrote 283 "Shadow" novels. He did it in seven consecutive years, writing one novel every two weeks. That equals about 120 finished pages each week.

Agatha Christie wrote eighty-five books, seventeen plays, fifteen films, and more than one hundred short stories.

Michael Avallone wrote 184 novels from 1953 to 1980, with over forty million copies being in print. He once finished a novel in one and a half days.

If you feel more depressed than inspired by such statistics, do not feel alone. Most writers will feel the same way until they reassess their own writing goals. We are not necessarily looking to produce a plethora of novels and short stories. At least some of us are concerned for nonfiction that takes research and planning. Many writers would rather produce a few quality titles than a glut of mediocre books. Not much polish and revision goes into a book that is written in a day and a half.

The purpose for our giving these statistics is only to point out that you *can* write a book if you really want to.

We know. The kids are crying; the phone is ringing; the relatives are coming for a visit; your stack of work from the office is piled up nearly to the sky. . . . The list is endless. But think about it this way. If you produce just one worthy typewritten page per day for two hundred days, then you will have a two-hundred page book in about six and a half months. Put that way, it doesn't sound so hard, does it?

In the next chapters we want to introduce you to some of the ideas of real, honest-to-goodness writers and editors. We want you to see how they think, work, and conduct their business. Learning that will help you follow a successful pattern of writing and publishing.

CHAPTER 3
What Writers Do and Why They Do It, Part 1

One element that we have striven for in this book is realism. We do not want to discourage writers by painting a picture of insurmountable odds and sacrifices that seem unending. Neither do we want to develop a rosy notion that writing is easy and publication is a snap. The fact is that writing for publication takes enormous work and developed skills. But—and keep this in mind throughout this book—*these skills and work habits can be learned.*

Drawing from our experiences as writers and editors, we developed nine questions that we put to a varied group of successful writers. You will recognize some of these names while others will be new to you. All were chosen because they are women and men who have committed themselves to the difficult task of learning to write. That makes their advice valuable. They have done what they suggest others do. With that in mind, let us look at their responses to our questions about the writing life.

1. What moved you to begin writing?

Ask ten writers how they started, and you will get ten different answers. We know because we did. The writers we surveyed come from a wide background of interests, work history, genre specialization, and experience; but they all share some common motivations and goals.

Alan Maki is a pastor and a writer. Like many writers, Maki found his interest as a child. "I began writing seriously at age nine and ten, when I wrote a 350-page book of short stories! I couldn't wait to go home after school, sit at my desk, and create magic on a piece of paper. It was something that felt like it was just in me. Creativity was so fun for me, and to this day (more than forty years later), I still feel the juices flowing when I write. After four published novels and writing seven hundred songs, I guess I'd have to continue to report that writing is something I just have to do. I'm happiest when I have one or two projects going." He also acknowledges the influence of an early teacher who wrote on one of his early short stories, "Keep up this kind of writing. It may turn into something someday." It has.

Jan Coleman likewise found her passion for words early in life. She notes that discovering books changed her life. "Reading as a child, I started with the Wizard of Oz books, every horse book ever published, and later many classics like *Jane Eyre, Wuthering Heights,* and books by Jane Austen and Charles Dickens. At age ten, after reading *Little Women,* I adapted the book into a play that we— my neighborhood pals—produced in my garage with me as the director. From the time I heard my words (paraphrased from Louisa May Alcott's) spoken from a script, I was convinced writing was my calling. I entered every writing contest from grade school on and won them all, especially the coveted privilege of writing our senior high musical."

Stephen Clark is a writer, editor, and Web site designer who says that writing fits the way God has made him. "I grew up with a love of words. As a kid I always had a paperback book in the hip pocket of my jeans. As soon as I learned how to read, I read all the time. In elementary school I'd take a book out to recess and sit against the building reading. At times the teachers actually took my book away and made me play! Of all the things there were to do or become, writing fits my personality best, so I guess that means God knows what He's doing." Clark, too, was fortunate to have been encouraged and mentored by his high school senior English teacher, who recognized and nurtured his talent, and his college academic advisor who, as he puts it, "prodded me forward."

Early influences also affected Vicki Caruana, a writer and educational consultant. She says of these influences, "For as long as I can remember, I process everything I experience through writing. Beginning with journals as a young girl, to fiction and poetry as a young woman, to communicating what I've learned as an adult, I write to understand my world better and to be understood. The turn to becoming a full-time writer came after a professor challenged me to write for an academic journal. I did, and I haven't stopped since!"

Ted Baehr feels he was born to be a writer. "My parents were stars of stage and screen. My father Ted Baehr's stage name was Bob 'Tex' Allen; he starred in more than fifty-one movies and in many Broadway plays. My mother's stage name was Evelyn Peirce; she starred in some of the first talking movies. Thus, I was born in the proverbial trunk on Broadway in New York City while my father was the juvenile lead in *Showboat,* and I had to write my way out of the show, as they say. One essay in the sixth grade was well received, and so I found writing to be a natural and enjoyable profession."

Kathi Macias' earliest memories include writing. She says, "I've wanted to write since I was a little girl. I've always been an avid reader, and when I was young I was sick a lot, so I had much more time to read. I read everything I could get my hands on, and when I ran out of things to read, I started writing my own stories. When I was in the second grade I wrote a story about Easter. My teacher liked it so much that she showed it to the principal, and they decided to turn it into a play for the PTA. It was very well received, and I was hooked.

Cecil Murphey is a successful writer who, like many others, began to learn early in life that words have power. He realized that he had some ability with words even as a youngster. He says, "I can't remember when I didn't want to write. Like many others in this profession, I had a miserable childhood. Reading and going to movies were the two outlets that showed me how wonderful the world could be."

Murphey explains, "As early as second grade, teachers told me I expressed myself well. When I was in seminary, my professors said I wrote excellent papers. Although I liked the compliments, I never thought my writing was exceptional. I made a few attempts to publish and they were rejected, so I didn't try to pursue writing. However, I couldn't get away from wanting to write. A year after seminary, I wrote an article, mailed it out (after revising it a total of eighteen times), and within a month a magazine accepted it. That first sale made me suspect that I could write." He never said writing is easy, which it is not, but he did find the courage to keep at it until he got the results he wanted.

Another writer who felt the tug of words early is Jerry "Chip" MacGregor. He is a writer, an agent representing some of the most successful writers in Christian publishing, and editor. When asked what moved him to begin writing, MacGregor says, "I've always been a words guy. I started writing as a child and never stopped. My mom says that when I was in first grade I came home and announced, 'When I grow up, I'm going to be a writer.' So I guess I had to live up to that promise. I've been writing ever since. My life has been intertwined with words. My first real job in college was as a copy editor for a junior high science teacher's magazine. I later worked for newspapers, then back to magazines, and eventually to books. I can't not write. There are stories inside me, or stories I see, and they simply must be told."

After reading thus far, you might be thinking, *Oh no, it's too late for me. I didn't start early enough.* Actually, beginning any time is soon enough. The key is to begin. Some successful writers experienced a rather late start.

Susan Titus Osborn is one such writer. Osborn is well-known as both a writer and a teacher of writers. She explains her start as follows: "I was teaching Sunday school at the time in 1978. I started using some of my own fiction stories to complement the Bible stories. The kids loved them, and a writer friend encouraged me to send them to church school take-home papers. I did, and my writing career was born. In 1984 I attended my first writers' conference at Biola University. The Standard Publishing editor knew I wrote take-home papers for her company, and she gave me the opportunity to write my first book. I've averaged a book a year since then, and to date, I've authored twenty-eight books."

Ken Walker, a successful freelance writer, did not begin in elementary school like some others, but he did begin to get the "bug" in high school and then pursued his career afterwards.

> Originally my interest in sports led to a part-time job in high school covering sports for the city newspaper in my hometown. After graduating from college in 1973, I held jobs at newspapers in four cities over the next nine years before making a transition to public relations with the Denver office of a major firm. However, after getting downsized during a slump in the oil business, I set up business as a one-man shop with part-time help for distribution of press releases and handling large accounts. I did some freelance writing on the side, particularly for a large oil and gas magazine; but this work dwindled as I got busier with PR work.

> That all came to a screeching halt in the fall of 1987 when the stock market took its biggest one-day dive in history. Within two months most of my business was gone. After several months of prayer, fasting, and agonizing over the future as the bills piled up, one day in my office I sensed God say softly, "I want you to use your writing talent for me." That was early in 1988, but things didn't get better. I closed my office in September and took a part-time job driving a delivery truck while ghostwriting testimonies for a Christian

businessmen's magazine. After being laid off in the spring of 1990, I went back to writing full-time and slowly built up my list of steady accounts.

You may find that your interest in writing is similar to these writers, or it may be very different. The key is to be yourself an develop your own gifts.

2. What kept (keeps) you going through the setbacks and disappointments? What were some of the major obstacles you had to overcome?

Even the most successful writers encounter problems that seem to stop them in their tracks. Some people simply give up while others find creative paths around the roadblocks. The answers we received to this question vary from person to person, but all believe that their faith in God has helped them overcome the temptation to quit.

Vicki Caruana uses her setbacks as opportunities to grow. "I believe that my ability to communicate through the written word is a gift from God. Learning how to be a good steward of that gift keeps me learning about the craft and polishing what I produce. I boast that it took seventy rejections before a magazine editor finally said yes to me. That was after years writing for a newspaper and taking the *Writer's Digest* correspondence course for nonfiction. I still get rejections for both articles and book proposals, but I believe nothing is wasted and that God redeems it all for his sake."

Ken Walker says that his sense of call to be a writer keeps him going.

That call from God is the only thing that keeps me going at times, since the setbacks and disappointments are numerous. In some ways, I'm still recovering from the financial collapse of 1987, and not having a steady income is at times a gut-wrenching ordeal. Yet this has deepened my faith in God since I have seen him provide in so many ways and at times when survival seemed impossible. As for disappointments, in spite of a desire to write more books, these opportunities have come sporadically; and numerous deals have fallen apart along the way. Also, after pouring one's heart into a project and investing a considerable amount of time, to watch the market make a collective yawn is disheartening. The sales and financial returns on my books have been extremely minimal.

Things began to improve for Walker when he began to add prayer to his work. "Probably the largest obstacle in the early days was finding steady outlets for writing. I had some, but my other efforts at selling additional, unsolicited copy was miserable. I rarely connected and struggled even to sell reprints. This all changed after I attended a writers' conference in March 1994, and one workshop leader suggested we get a prayer team to support our ministry. I found five people to pray over a list of monthly projects I sent them, and by July of that year my work literally exploded. I knew I hadn't suddenly become brilliant, so this was an obvious answer to prayer."

Uneven income is an obstacle many writers face. Ken Walker tells how he deals with this issue. "I would never recommend anyone set out to try full-time writing without some form of financial reserves or a working spouse. My wife found a nice-paying job while I was in the worst of my transition, and for a while after I returned to full-time writing, and without her income we would have starved. Survival is the main objective. One can't write well while worried about paying the mortgage, utilities, and grocery bills."

Some of the difficulties writers face can be personal. Susan Titus Osborn had such obstacles. "In 1987 I went through a terrible divorce. Until that time I had thought of my writing as an avocation, and I didn't even consider making a living at it. I got down on my knees and prayed, 'Lord, can I make a living writing?' His answer was yes. He opened doors for me to start a critique service where I could help others learn to write and to run a large writers' conference. He provided the funds so I could finish my BA in religious studies and obtain an MA in communications. All the while I grabbed free moments to write books. He truly turned my avocation into a vocation."

Osborn says of her personal story, "I also have a history of back problems, but I've learned to pace myself. I get up from the computer often and stretch. If the pain is bad, since I work at home, I can lie down for a while. I've also developed heart problems and glaucoma, but I've learned to manage both through modern medicine. I've learned to write no matter what."

Jan Coleman had some similar experiences of setbacks and roadblocks.

> Looking back, I'm surprised that I wasn't
> encouraged more by my high school teachers and

counselors to focus on writing as a career, but back in my day—late sixties—women went for teaching or nursing, and I cringed at the thought of either. My grandmother was an unpublished writer, but she left me a box of manuscripts, articles, and stories from her life. She told me that I had the talent and I'd be the writer in the family. In college I majored in drama but fell in love and got married before finishing. A difficult marriage kept me from pursuing my dream of publishing, but I never stopped writing and storing my scribbling for "someday." My grandmother's legacy kept me going. I wanted to fulfill her dream for me.

Coleman began moving toward her long-delayed dream even though she could not see where it would lead.

I collected writing books, though I couldn't relate that much because I wasn't actually submitting, but I took creative writing classes and knew somehow that my day would come. I had my first story published as a result of a writing for children's workshop. When we moved to the country (toward the end of my marriage), I boldly offered myself as a stringer for the weekly newspaper for five cents an inch—though I had never written feature articles. I studied past issues and put my skills to work. I would have paid them to let me do it. I learned the newspaper business from typesetting to ad copy to editing. After my divorce I hated leaving for a "real" job in the city.

Coleman faced one obstacle that many before and since have encountered—lack of self-confidence and fear of failure. "I'd bragged to my high school graduating class, after the success of the senior musical, that they would someday be asking for my autograph on books. I didn't publish my first book until after I turned fifty."

Cecil Murphey, like many before him, felt he could not make it as a writer, so he decided to quit. He says, "At least three times I've decided to quit writing, but I've always come back. I keep having new ideas that won't leave me alone. Somewhere between pain and disappointment comes the sense that God has called me to write. I published at least a dozen articles before I realized that all serious writers face rejection and disappointment. That didn't ease the pain, but it did help me begin to understand that editors rejected the product and not the writer."

Some writers, like Alan Maki, use obstacles as an added incentive to try harder. He says, "As a writer I simply worked hard, believed in my abilities, and fought through the obstacles. Yes, there are obstacles, particularly rejection slips. Once a writer understands that rejection is part of the process, it's not so tough to deal with it. I've received enough rejection slips to wallpaper a couple of rooms in my house, but I was determined not to be stopped. The four book contracts I've signed look pretty good against that backdrop. Bottom line: obstacles are just a part of life. If you have talent mixed with perseverance, you will succeed some of the time."

Kathi Macias realizes that obstacles confront everyone who wants to write. She says, "Because I am not an 'expert' in a particular field—counseling, finance, etc.— I didn't have the readymade niche that some writers have.

However, my passion is not just to write about a specific field, but rather about anything that pertains to Jesus, so that keeps me on track, willing to fight through the obstacles that inevitably come along."

Stephen Clark sees one issue Christian writers face is the fear of not developing God-given talent as it should be. "For a Christian writer I believe that we have a much higher standard to live up to. If we are writing of the things of God, that is an awesome responsibility, and we need to take it seriously." In addition to that, he notes that some mundane issues creep into a writer's path. "There are the usual issues of making the time to write and ignoring distractions."

Chip MacGregor offers a unique perspective on the matter of challenges and setbacks.

> I suppose a lot of writers will tell you that writing is therapy—and I suppose it is for me in a way. But I've kept writing because I still have stories to tell. I rarely feel that the setbacks I've faced were because of my writing. Rather, they were in spite of my writing, or at odds with my writing. So I kept writing until I could convince the people who made the mistake of saying no in the first place. And let's face it—most disappointment authors face is really the simple act of rejection. Writers hate to hear the word *no*. But I've never been one who allowed no to get in the way of accomplishing what I wanted. So while I've had more than my share of no's, I've continued writing because that's what I do.

MacGregor realizes that a rejection is not the end of the world or a repudiation of his career. "The fact that some publisher doesn't want to purchase my words doesn't mean they lack value. I don't expect the act of publishing to validate my life. My words are meaningful. They are my ministry, even if they are only meant as a ministry to myself, or my wife, or the authors I represent. I continue writing in the face of rejection simply because that's who I am. I must continue writing."

For Marvin Olasky, a professor of journalism and a much-published writer, adversity can make a writer stronger. He notes that the factor that keeps him going, even despite turndowns, is simple: "Faith in God." He says that the early obstacles were getting turned down by publishers. Now some of his dilemmas include finding time to write. Many writers identify with both of these obstacles.

Stephen Clark says that someone who has writing as a part of his or her makeup simply cannot help but work despite the obstacles. "I have to write. I am a writer. I love it (and sometimes hate it too). I know it is my calling. It's what I'm skilled at and what gives me satisfaction."

The writers who have shared their perspectives thus far have painted a picture of a calling with real setbacks but real victories too. Anything worth doing, especially writing, is worth counting the cost and then attacking with vigor. Let us go back to our professionals and ask more questions about their backgrounds and their work.

3. If you were beginning today, what would you hope to accomplish?

Many writers, even seasoned veterans, still feel like they are beginners in the sense of wanting to keep learning and finding new ways of overcoming hurdles. In fact, many have come to realize the irony of having experience: the minute you think you have arrived is the minute you begin to lose your edge.

Pastor and writer Alan Maki offers a realistic perspective about beginning and accomplishing goals.

> I still feel like a beginner today. Every project is fresh and new and makes me feel like I'm just beginning. In fact, even though I've got some books out there, I've been rejected a couple of times since. I now have one of my books being produced as a movie, but that doesn't make me a veteran who automatically will succeed again. I have to work just as hard as ever and fight through the same obstacles that exist for every writer. I'm currently working on another book and a screenplay, which excites me like a fifteen-year-old kid, but I have no guarantees. I'm just a beginner on new projects, but I've fought the good fight and have a bit of seasoning which I can depend on.

Vicki Caruana also thinks of herself as a beginner each day. She says, "To me every day is a new beginning. I want to write not what the market says I should write but what I believe God is leading me to write. After authoring more than eighty articles and eighteen books, I now know what I want to do. I have stories to tell. That's my focus now."

When asked what she would like to accomplish if starting over, Jan Coleman offers another realistic answer. "The same as I've already accomplished, writing a life-changing book. In the past, before being published, I only dreamed of writing fiction. I started a dozen novels—as my strongest suit was living in fantasy of my life. I never imagined writing nonfiction books for women drawing on my personal pain, but I see how my newspaper training and years working as a legislative aide for the California State Senate as a writer prepared me for it."

Accomplishing the will of God is the overall goal of most writers. Stephen Clark says his goal is "Whatever is God's will for me to accomplish with my writing. Of course, I'd love to write a best-selling work, but only if it really honored the Lord—not just to make money." Ken Walker echoes these sentiments, stating what he would do if he were starting over, "Probably the same as now, which is to write about God's work in the world."

Some writers look back and marvel over what they have already been able to achieve. Susan Titus Osborn is one such author and teacher. She observes:

> I have accomplished more than I ever dreamed. People are always telling me how much my books have touched their lives or how they have learned to polish their writing through my writing books, e-mail course, and the classes I teach at conferences. I think the legacy I will leave behind is the knowledge I have imparted to others to help them improve their writing and to encourage them to persevere. I hope other writers keep their eyes on their readers and what they can do to encourage them, improve their lives, and bring them closer to God.

This is a great reminder that what we achieve is not for ourselves alone.

Chip MacGregor also recognizes that helping others, and not just self-expression, is the goal of Christian writers. Because of that, he would still try to reach out to others. "I'd still like the world to be different because of my words. I like to educate, to assist, to enlighten, to entertain. The body of my words is meant to take people a bit further along the path so that they better understand who they are, who we are as people, how we are to live in light of truth."

Ted Baehr has a ready answer when asked what he would do if he were beginning his writing career over. "I would have focused on screenwriting. As it is, however, I rejoice in God's grace made manifest in my attempts to communicate that part of his truth that he has called me to communicate." He notes that movies and television have powerful opportunities to influence large numbers of people—thus his interest in those media.

One of the most commercially successful writers interviewed for this book, Cecil Murphey, answers questions about his goals if he were beginning today with his usual humility. "My goals would be the same today as they were when I started: I wrote simply because I felt compelled to write and wanted to see my work published. For the first two years, I struggled to get all those ideas out of my head and onto paper. I also learned that when we push the old ones out, new ideas sneak in. I didn't plan to be a full-time writer. I was a pastor and wrote for thirteen years before I jumped into full-time writing. In fact, for several years, I thought I had the perfect career as a pastor, a part-time writer, and a part-time instructor at a Bible college."

4. How can a beginning writer acquire the technical skills necessary to become a published author and successful in any genre?

One of the most important things for a beginning writer to do is to develop the technical skills that are necessary for success. By "technical skills" we mean correct spelling, excellent grammar, and adequate research skills. For the most part, these elements of writing are not the favorites of most people, but they are vital. Some writers think such mundane matters are beneath their concern. But think about it this way. Would you hire a carpenter to build your house who did not care about the quality of his tools, quality of his screws and nails, and the grade of lumber he used?

The technical skills addressed here are the tools writers use to build their writing. Yes, this can sometimes be tedious and even boring, but when you work to master these matters, they become more or less second nature so you do not need to spend precious time trying to remember how to spell *righteous* or wondering about the rules for split infinitives.

Let us now consider the perspectives of some experienced writers. Their advice may save you many headaches.

Cecil Murphey speaks for many writers when he warns, "We need to learn the craft. That means hard work." He points out that writing can be learned if the novice writer will spend the effort and time to get the basics. Murphey says, "When I started to write, I didn't know of any writers conferences, but I now urge beginning writers to attend them. Although it didn't appeal to me, many have benefited from correspondence courses." Early in his career he did three things that he recommends to every writer.

1. *Read about writing.* Our local library had thirty-one books on writing, and I began to check them out, one at a time, and read each one. I subscribed to two writers magazines. I wanted to learn from people who had become successful.

2. *Join or start an editing group.* I started an editing group back in the 1970s when we had to type carbon copies of everything. We never read aloud, which I think is a waste of time. We edited one another's manuscripts at home and gave fifteen minutes of oral feedback in our meetings. It was a lot of work for all of us. We learned to write better while learning to edit one another. Those who weren't serious about their writing dropped out. Two of us from the group, which lasted nine years, became full-time writers, and one became a full-time editor.

3. *Read everything by writers you like.* I wasn't always sure why I liked particular writers, but I assumed they attracted me by their writing style as well as their content. As I read, I'd ask, "Why did you say it that way?" I still carry on a dialogue with the writers and occasionally write notes or arguments in the margins.

Another full-time writer, Ken Walker, considers the issue of technical skills and concludes with Murphey that there is only one way to master them—by plain old-fashioned hard work. "There is no easy answer to this question. It starts with a basic education, which goes back to fifth or sixth grade, and learning how to diagram sentences. If you don't understand the basics of grammar, nouns and verbs, then I don't see how you can expect to write fluently. In addition, you must be a voracious reader if you expect to write. Saying you don't want to read because you don't want anyone to influence your writing is like saying you want to become a race car driver but don't want to watch any races because you'd hate for those experts to teach you anything."

Walker notes that once you begin to master the basic tools of writing, you can move on to other elements of the profession.

> Find a writers group in your area. Many are listed in *Writers Market* and the *Christian Writers Market Guide,* or online. A writer needs the camaraderie of other writers, the feedback from critique groups, and other intangibles a group offers. Make plans to attend a writers conference; they are becoming more common all over the nation. If a green beginner, you may want to start with an event in your area that doesn't cost too much, but eventually you need to attend a several-day event where there will be numerous editors and writers on the faculty. I sold my first commercial book to an editor I met at Mount Hermon, and with more publishers closed to unsolicited submissions, conferences are a valuable place to meet editors, make connections, and get educated.

A writer must also keep working to stay up with trends and understand the changes in the publishing industry.

Walker says, "There is also the matter of ongoing education, such as reading *Writer's Digest, The Christian Communicator,* or other writing publications, buying copies of market guides and other directories and books that cover specific topics of interest. Too many writers think they can just go to the computer and start writing without investing time or effort in acquiring knowledge or necessary tools of the trade."

Susan Titus Osborn believes that one good way to learn writing skills is by meeting people who actually write and learn from them. That is one reason conferences are so valuable. She also says, "A writer can take e-mail courses such as we offer through the Christian Communicator Manuscript Critique Service. A listing of all conferences and writing helps is listed in Sally Stuart's *Christian Writers' Market Guide.*"

Vicki Caruana echoes this need for working hard to develop good skills. Too often beginners think they do not need to worry about the basics because all that is important is the story. But that is not the case. Caruana observes, "I am a teacher for the Christian Writers Guild, and I find that many new writers believe they don't have to gain the technical skills—that their message or story is good enough. Our goal should be to become writers of excellence. Our work should stand apart from the rest of what's out there. Enroll in a writing course. Hone your grammar skills. Read great writing. Do whatever it takes to become the best you can be."

Several writers consulted for this book suggest that a good way to gain technical skill is by writing for a local newspaper. Marvin Olasky says it will help the writer "at observing specific detail." Jan Coleman notes that writing for the newspaper has several advantages. It will help teach the regular crafting of words and a professional attitude toward the work. "If possible, ask your local newspaper if you can submit personal interest stories, profiles of interesting people in the community. Do it for free if necessary or for whatever they'll pay. Write about people for magazines, Sunday school take-home papers, whoever will print what you write in the beginning. You'll learn to hone your skills—crafting good leads, setting the scene, describing characters, writing dialogue—plus, you have to learn to narrow your focus and write tight, two things most beginning writers neglect, because we love the sound of our own words."

For Kathi Macias the training she received in journalism provided a sound foundation. She observes, "My best training was the time I spent studying journalism. It taught me to write 'on command,' 'on time,' and 'on target.' I've never regretted those studies, though I never desired a career in journalism itself. I would strongly advise that sort of training to any aspiring writers looking for direction. In addition, for those who are looking to write fiction I would advise taking classes in drama. That was a huge help to me in learning how to develop three-dimensional characters and believable dialogue."

Many seasoned writers have attitudes that might sound stiff or even harsh. But they have learned that nothing worthwhile is ever easy. All valuable skills are learned the old-fashioned way—through hard work.

Alan Maki's advice has the ring of authenticity to it because he has developed the basic skills through extensive labor. Maki says, "I think you need to have grammar and spelling skills and an ability to put great thoughts on paper. In other words, you have to have a lot in place with which to begin. Since only 2 percent or less of all would-be authors ever get published, you must come into the game with a talent that appears undeniable, even if in need of polish. You must want it badly, or else the work and overcoming obstacles is too hard, time-consuming, and not worth the pain. Bottom line: a beginning writer needs to get his/her hands on numerous books for writers and study them. Also, a beginning writer needs to understand that the key to 'getting good' is rewriting, rewriting, and rewriting. If you are not willing to rewrite until the cows come home, don't even start. Find another pursuit."

Stephen Clark realizes that everything about the writing life, even the technical issues, has a spiritual dimension. The Christian writer is under even more of an obligation to practice the craft well and develop a God-honoring mind-set. Clark says:

> For a Christian writer, especially one that is writing about specifically Christian and biblical things, I think he/she has the responsibility not only to master the typical writing skills but also continuously to seek to study the Bible (beyond daily devotions and Sunday sermons), theology, Christian history, philosophy, sociology, and more.

> A Christian writer to be truly honoring to God and truly effective needs to develop a clear and sharp Christian mind-set and worldview.

> Otherwise, theological error will creep into your writing, which means you could be influencing others to think and act contrary to

what God intended. It's an awesome responsibility to be a Christian writer, and it takes more than going to a few writers seminars!

Ted Baehr is interested in screenwriting. He advises beginning writers to focus on their area of interest and master it. Regarding writing for the screen, Baehr says, "Read and write without ceasing. Study the craft, and study the great writers." He offers several seminal works on writing drama:

Lajos Egri. *The Art of Dramatic Writing: Its Basis in the Creative Interpretation of Human Motives*. New York: Simon and Schuster, 1960.

Robert McKee. *Story: Substance, Structure, Style, and the Principles of Screenwriting*. New York: Regan Books, 1997.

Linda Seger. *Making a Good Script Great*. New York: Samuel French Trade, 1994.

Veteran writer and agent Chip MacGregor has thought deeply about the motivation for writers to master and practice their craft. Too many, he notes, do not want to master a craft at all. They simply want the recognition that comes from writing. "I believe most new writers basically want to get published so that they'll be famous. They want that thrill of holding up a book with their name emblazoned on the cover, show it to their friends, leave it on their coffee table, maybe peruse a copy at the bookstore, and casually mention to someone in the aisle, 'I wrote that.' I think most new writers are seeking fame and encouragement, that they believe validity and meaning will arrive out of publication. They see fame as offering a measurable amount of worth and competence."

The irony of this situation is that many writers get better and better at their craft and leave behind the idea of recognition and fame. MacGregor says: "Most writers who have achieved some level of fame (and forgive me for including myself in this select company) fairly quickly eschew it in favor of craft. We may still enjoy the warmth associated with being recognized or having someone come up to us and praise our words. But most successful authors discover that fame is not only fleeting; it doesn't make us better people or better writers. And that, I think, is why so many successful writers I know spend considerable time attempting to improve their craft."

MacGregor realizes that these statements may seem extreme to some people. "If that's true (and it might be too much of a leap for readers to accept), then the one thing beginning writers ought to do is to devote themselves to improving their craft of writing. As an agent, I see hundreds of manuscripts every year that I reject for representation. Nearly all of these are rejected for one basic reason: the writer simply isn't good enough. Their ideas may be interesting, and their marketing may be slick, but the authors simply aren't good enough to publish. That's a message I've tried to get into the heads of beginning writers everywhere: Don't try seeking the secret of writing. Improve as a writer. I've yet to meet a great writer who is not published.

"And how does one go about doing that? I don't think it's all that complicated—write regularly and expose yourself to great writing. A beginning writer should read widely and should focus on great, not popular, writing. A beginning writer should set aside time to write regularly and should make writing a habit in his or her life. Beginning writers should find someone who can help them improve—a writing instructor, a writing mentor, an experienced editor, even a writing critique group, so long as the members can bring some wisdom to bear on the issue of craft."

The idea of being published can be seductive. The temptation is for novices to try to launch their work too early. MacGregor observes:

> I know of no other craft that promotes beginners before they are ready. Surely a young pianist doesn't take a couple of lessons and rent a concert hall to present Rachmaninoff's "Rhapsody on a Theme by Paganini." A first-year ballet student doesn't expect to dance the role of the Sugar Plum Fairy. An artist cannot expect to move directly from paint-by-numbers to creating fine portraits. Yet I often meet beginning writers who are determined to publish something. They often have no clue of their motivation or message (though they can dress it up with God-talk and make it sound like "a calling"). My advice to beginning writers is to study the craft of writing by reading and listening to those who already know it, in order to become more like them.

MacGregor continues:

> Beginning writers must understand that all writing is derivative. I recently read a biography of the Beatles, in which George Harrison spoke of listening to Chuck Berry records and imitating his riffs, then trying to find a place to incorporate those notes into songs the Beatles were performing. As he grew as an artist, Harrison realized that other up-and-coming guitarists were

imitating him. Yet he realized that his own playing was a derivative of Chuck Berry, who had derived his own style from listening to Chet Atkins, who was himself a derivative of Leadbelly. In fact, any exploration of the etymology of modern music will reveal a clear pattern of derivation. Writing is similar.

To illustrate how the process of learning to write actually works, MacGregor tells of the following incident. In 1919, a young man who had been injured in the war in Europe moved to Chicago, picking one particular neighborhood in order to be close to the noted author Sherwood Anderson. The young writer, impressed with the critical praise heaped on Anderson's *Winesburg, Ohio,* had heard the novelist was willing to assist beginning writers. The two men became close. They met every day to read together, exploring the writing of newspapers and magazines, and eventually tearing apart the inner workings of novels.

The young man brought his own work to Anderson, who helped him see how he could improve his craft. Anderson even introduced the young writer to his network of publishing associates and helped him publish his first novel, which was met with critical acclaim. Its title was *The Sun Also Rises.* The young man's name was Ernest Hemingway.

Sherwood Anderson then moved to New Orleans, where he took another young author through those same paces, even putting up $300 of his own money to help that beginning writer's first novel get published. That novel was entitled *Soldier Pay.* The author's name was

William Faulkner. Anderson would then move to California, where he worked with a young writer by the name of John Steinbeck.

Sherwood Anderson shaped modern American writing more profoundly than any author except Mark Twain. Most of the writing instructors of the late twentieth century were, in one way or another, disciples of Anderson. And the reason Sherwood Anderson was so committed to mentoring beginning writers? Perhaps it was because, when he was young, a more experienced author by the name of Theodore Dreiser had invested in his own life and craft.

MacGregor concludes, "I think that's the answer to your question: beginning writers must find a Sherwood Anderson to help them develop."

Not every writer may have the opportunity to find a Sherwood Anderson to serve as a mentor, but every writer can develop the necessary skills to improve. You are reading this book as such an effort.

In the next chapter we continue to offer the advice, experience, and perspective of this group of seasoned writers. We believe their experience is a useful tool in blazing a path through what can look like a jungle otherwise known as the publishing industry.

CHAPTER 4
What Writers Do and Why They Do It, Part 2

In this chapter we continue an interview with a group of writers about various aspects of writing and the life of writers.

5. How do you actually write, that is, what is your personal process of researching and writing? Can you write anywhere, anytime, or do you prefer specific locations, times, environments, etc.?

One of the many facets of writing that seem to trouble beginning writers is the issue of translating thought to disk and beyond. How does a writer find the time—more properly—*make* the time to write? What is the process of doing the research and then forming it into a usable whole? Do writers prefer to work in long blocks of uninterrupted time or in short spurts? What locations work best—home office, professional studio, or something else?

We asked many writers these sorts of questions and, as we expected, got many different answers. The reason for such varied responses is that writing is an intensely personal craft. What works for one person may not work for another. Even so, their responses might help open a window to the process of getting words into print.

Susan Titus Osborn sketches her method of creating a piece from the origin of the idea to the edited manuscript:

> I start with an idea that pops into my head. I develop it into a focus sentence and make a rough outline. These ideas come to me when I'm driving, doing something totally unrelated, and sleeping. I need to pull off the road or get up and jot enough down so the idea doesn't leave me. Then I can develop it when I have some free time, preferably the next day.
>
> When I sit down to write a first rough draft though, I try to pick a time when I am at my best and when I won't have any interruptions. Then I just sit down and type with no thought to editing as I go. After I get some distance between myself and the "baby" I've created, then I go back and edit what I have written. I can edit while my husband is driving down the road or with a commotion going on in my house; but for the first drafts and conceptualizing ideas, I need total concentration. Editing is the longest part of the process and the place where beginners fall down on the job. They don't work hard and long enough on their creation to bring it up to publishing standards.

Vicki Caruana focuses on the task at hand to determine exactly how the process might need to proceed. She says:

When I begin a new nonfiction topic, I first create an outline of the concepts I plan to cover. Then I immerse myself in research on that topic. Much of what I've written relies on Scripture teaching, so I go into what I call "Bible study mode" for the entire time it takes to write the book. I write every day, no matter what. It could be two hundred words, or it could be a thousand words, but I write nevertheless. You have to train your mind to respond when you sit down in the same place, often at the same time. But there have been times when it has been difficult for me to write. Life changes get in the way; and when that happens, I immerse myself only in the Lord, and then slowly I emerge able to write again.

Some people might be surprised to learn how "ordinary" writing can be. Jan Coleman, for example, speaks of her process of writing as simply "going to work." She offers this explanation.

I keep office hours just like I did working downtown. I show up at the same time and write until five o'clock in my home office. I've surrounded myself with things that encourage me. On the wall I have a wooden sign that says, "Imagine." I've framed my book covers for wall art. I love films, so I've bought lobby posters of my favorite movies, and I have one wall of bookcases filled with writing books, quote books (I collect them from everywhere), travel books (my other passion), my favorite fiction, Bibles and commentaries, and research books on World

War II, the sixties, and Vietnam because I've got two novels in progress. My "someday" projects.

Coleman further explains, "I can write in other environments with a laptop and access to the Internet for research, and a good thesaurus; but I'm not one who can write in snatches at Starbucks. I research extensively before I start a project, when I'm in the book proposal or magazine query stage. I frequent used bookstores in every town I visit, snooping for books on subjects of interest to me, and I have favorite Internet sources. Organization is not my strong suit, so I have to force myself to sort the information into files. I'm a messy worker, papers and books piled everywhere. Somehow I've learned to work this way, but to others it looks like impossible chaos."

Stephen Clark shares the following method of work. "It varies depending on what I'm tackling. But generally I do best when I can manage to arrange large blocks of uninterrupted time, especially when the writing is more creative. But, thanks to having worked under Bob Walker who founded *Christian Life* magazine and others, I learned how to write fast and well under deadlines. When I have to, I can write just about anywhere. Also, having worked in corporate communications, I've learned how to write on the spot when a news release had to go out ASAP. I adjust based on what I need to accomplish."

Kathi Macias simply does not let petty annoyances stop her work. She says, "I can write wherever and whenever the opportunity presents itself. I prefer my quiet office with my familiar and well broken-on computer, but I can scribble on napkins in a restaurant if need be. At the same time, I don't believe in waiting until 'the muse whispers,' nor do I believe in writer's block. In fact I have a piece of wood in my office with the words 'writer's block' stenciled on it. When I find myself stumped as to where to go next on a writing assignment, I simply turn the block over and get back to work!"

Ken Walker, another professional writer, speaks of his daily schedule that works well for him.

> I work out of a home office that has all the tools of an office—computer, desks, Internet connection, phone, tape recorder, filing cabinet, lamps, office supplies, and so on. With everything on the Internet these days, I rarely go to the library. When I did once several years back, they pointed me to their computer—research I could have done at home. (I still go to the library but mainly to find books I want to read or need for research. I can access the library's database through my computer and card number that gains me access.) So I research and write at the office during normal working hours as anyone at an office would, except my hours often extend until 6 or 6:30 in the evening. When I have assignments that take me on the road, I rarely have time to do much writing. Planes are so cramped I can't figure out where I would find space to spread out my notes and work on a computer. So rather than lugging along a laptop, I use whatever free time I have to catch up on the constant stack of reading I have to do.

Alan Maki says that a writer should develop a professional attitude about everything in the writing process, including the methods of making it happen. Maki says,

"Once I have a story in mind that just 'has to be written,' I do the necessary research and planning. When I have the total act together, I start to write. I'm a pastor, and since I have an office with a computer available for use for hours every day, I tend to find time to write in my office. I make time, whether in the morning or afternoon, during each day. But in all honesty it doesn't end there. Last night, in fact, I was up three times during the middle of the night with a movie scene that wouldn't wait until morning. I wrote madly with pen and paper so I wouldn't lose the dialogue before morning came. Also, I take the story home with me from my office so I can write for a few minutes here and there throughout the early evening, if family time permits. In other words, I'm ready at any time if the juices are flowing and cannot be denied. I don't allow myself to be unprepared when it's time."

Maki has another technique to finish a project. He says, "When a book deadline is drawing closer, if I'm a bit behind, I take a week and go to a cabin by myself to get a lot of writing done. I've done this three times, and it's worked well for me."

One of the most productive freelance writers working today, Cecil Murphey, experimented with several methods of working until he settled on a technique that works well for him.

> I can write anywhere and anytime. However, after becoming a full-time writer, I choose to write only at my desk. When I write, it begins with an idea; I allow that idea to float around inside my head until the material seeps or explodes. If I'm doing nonfiction, while ideas float I read anything remotely connected with the topic. With fiction

I don't want other books to influence me, so
I don't read in the genre where I'm planning
to write.

I don't start writing until I know the first
sentence. (I may edit that sentence three times
before I turn in my manuscript.) For me, once
I type those first words, the book or article begins
to fall into place. That happens on some kind of
unconscious level. As soon as I type my first
paragraph, the next comes and the next—at least
most of the time.

Usually, I'll finish the first chapter. By the time
I've finished the chapter, I seem to know how to
structure the book, and I type the outline.

Ted Baehr says that his mood sometimes dictates how
he writes. "I will write anywhere at any time, and I love
to type, scribble, and dictate, depending on the task and
my mood."

Veteran agent and writer Chip MacGregor made a dis-
covery years ago that helped revolutionize his concept of
how he goes about his work.

For years I tried writing in dribs and drags,
trying to get an actual "writing career" going.
I did quite a bit of magazine writing, but I could
never get over the hump and get a book done.
Then two articles I stumbled across in the course
of my reading changed my writing life.

The first was an interview with Thomas Wolfe
in *Esquire* magazine. Wolfe, the author of such
books as *The Right Stuff, The Bonfire of the
Vanities,* and *The Man in Full,* was shown

resplendent in a white suit, hat, and spats. The caption read, "Thomas Wolfe on his way to the office." Notably, his office was in his home. Wolfe would get up, get dressed, and go into a spare bedroom to write just as though he were heading off to an important publishing luncheon in a downtown New York restaurant. In the article Wolfe explained that, to him, writing was a business, so he treated it like a business. He would begin writing at nine every morning and would write until noon. Then he'd take ninety minutes off for lunch. Wolfe noted that he didn't wait for inspiration to strike him; instead, he would sit down, read the last few pages of what he'd written the day before, and begin to type. By simply approaching it as a business, he got much more done. After lunch he returned to his office to answer his mail (this being in that long-ago era before e-mail), return phone calls, and take care of any pressing business matters. When he was done, he would begin writing again. An alarm went off at 4:30, when he ended his day "attending to the business of writing."

The idea that writing was "a business" was an eye-opening thought to MacGregor. He continues:

That article was a revelation to me. The thought of approaching writing as a business had never occurred to me. I immediately changed my entire approach to writing. Though working full-time as a university administrator, I began getting up early and writing from six to eight every morning before going in to my day job. In short order I had my first book written. I soon figured out that for me the best plan was to have a place to write, a time to write, and a project to write on. Rather than waiting for my mood to be right and my muse to appear, I simply sat down each morning and started writing.

The second article that changed my life was a short biography of British novelist P. G. Wodehouse, creator of the characters Jeeves and his bumbling master, Bertie Wooster. Wodehouse was an unsuccessful salesman in the 1920s, when he decided to begin writing entertaining short stories to help make ends meet. As a young man, he set a goal: each day he would write eleven hundred salable words. He admitted that sometimes he would be done by one in the afternoon and would immediately stop writing and go play golf. Other days he wouldn't be done until one the next morning. But he kept at it, since eleven hundred words would allow him to make a living at writing. Over the course of a long career, Wodehouse published more than ninety novels, hundreds of short stories, and several stage plays. His simple goal made him one of the most published novelists of the twentieth century.

When I left academia to write full-time, I followed Wodehouse's method. I got up each morning, got dressed, ate breakfast, and went to my office (a spare bedroom in the house my wife and I were renting). There I would read the last few pages of my previous day's work, then begin typing. My goal was to create half a chapter per day—later that became a chapter per day, one of the reasons I've been able to produce more than fifty books and study guides before my fiftieth birthday.

I no longer write full-time, having decided to spend more time helping other writers as an agent and writing teacher, but I continue to write on special projects. And when I do, I still treat it the same way—I pick a time (generally first thing in the morning), a place (still a room in my house, preferably quiet and without many interruptions), and a project. I organize my thoughts and my notes, then I sit down and write.

MacGregor has what he calls three "tricks of the trade" that he believes will benefit all writers. He says:

All three of these have helped me immeasurably in my writing career. These are just tricks of the trade that I've learned from experience, and new writers may find them valuable. The first is to read your work out loud. I've never published anything that I haven't read to myself out loud in my writing room. That has helped me figure out when something I've written doesn't work. My ear will tell me I need to re-write it.

The second is that a beginning writer should learn the importance of writing a book or article all the way through. Whether you're creating a novel or a nonfiction book, get all the way through one draft before going back to sharpen and polish. The first draft may be awful, but

there's value in going through the process of
creating an entire book that you can't get by just
doing pieces of a book.

The third is that a writer need not suffer
writer's block if he or she will simply stop writing
and talk through it. Whenever I get stuck in one
place, I read what I've just written, push away
from my computer screen, and start talking out
loud. I act as though I'm teaching a class, and
since I generally know what I want to say, if
I start talking out loud, it will all come out. I'll
quickly figure out what I want to say next, and
soon I'm back at my screen, banging out words.

Marvin Olasky gives his method of writing via a poem
reminiscent of Dr. Seuss:

> I can write on a bus, even when there is a fuss.
> Dogs may be biting and people fighting,
> but I've learned to keep on writing.
> From the tip of my nose to the ends of my toes,
> I do so like green eggs and prose.

6. What do beginning writers need to know about the financial aspects of writing?

Some writers seem to believe that earning money from
writing is somehow unholy or at least unsavory. But think
about everything that goes into producing a book. A
person writes it, an editor works on it to put it into the
best shape possible, a company has to pay to have it
printed and bound, and a salesperson has to introduce
it to a bookstore. Then we hope someone buys it. Making

a commercially viable book requires many steps. Money is part of the process. Bringing even a small paperback book to market can cost between $10,000 and $20,000.

Determine you will learn all you can about the financial aspects of publishing so neither of two things will happen: (1) you will be taken advantage of, and (2) you will be unreasonable in your expectations regarding what you will earn.

The writers we interviewed for this book had varying perspectives on the issue of money and writing. Alan Maki's comments are typical of many experienced writers. "It's one thing to write a few books, but for those books to bring you hundreds of thousands of dollars is another thing. It doesn't happen to many people. Most writers have other jobs, as I do. I'm a pastor and love that job, as well. Over the past several years, my royalties from a few books amount to a few thousand dollars each year. That's nice, but I couldn't live on those checks. Initial advances are bigger, but they wouldn't keep me out of living in a cardboard box."

Jan Coleman realized early in her career that money would be tight. "When I left my job at the legislature, I knew we'd have to live without my salary, and that writing would probably never make up for that paycheck. I've had to readjust my lifestyle, shop at discount stores, and save money whenever I can. We chose to stay in our existing home rather than move across town where we'd like to be; that's a small price to pay for being able to live out my dream." Coleman cautions beginners to be realistic. Most writers hear early on not to do it for the money; it's not there for most of us. And it puts extreme pressure on the author to mass produce, and quality often suffers.

Stephen Clark is blunt in his assessment of the earning potential of most beginners: "Prepare for poverty!" But he explains his evaluation from his own experience. "Other than for a small number of writers, there is no fame, glamour, or wealth involved in writing. In fact, it seems that everyone and their brother are writers! Everyone thinks they can do it and do it well, and a lot of people can. To stand out above the crowd as a writer takes a tremendous talent. However, unlike many professions, a really good writer has many paths he or she can pursue and earn a decent living. When I worked at AT&T, more than one upper-level manager assured me that if I stayed with the corporation I'd always have a good paying job merely based on my skill as a writer."

Susan Titus Osborn echoes Clark's views. She notes, "Don't quit your day job! Although I currently have twelve books in print, I don't make a living off of them. The bulk of my income comes from my critique service and speaking at conferences, retreats, and churches where I sell my own books."

Chip MacGregor explains how he learned to think about the financial aspects of writing and what might help other writers.

> Only a few thousand people in this country make a full-time living at writing. Don't assume, just because you're hanging out at conferences with people who write books, that the world is made up of full-time writers. An average novelist may take eight to ten months to write a book. With time added for edits and galleys, that works out to about one novel per year. Yet that novelist, unless he or she has a breakout book, is no doubt

going to be paid less than $20,000 for the novel—sometimes considerably less. That means you'd work an entire year to scrimp by on wages barely above the poverty line. So think carefully before you quit your day job.

Here's what I did when I decided I wanted to write for a living: I set a monthly income goal for my writing. When I first started (on a part-time basis), my goal was to make $100 per month. I sold articles, wrote advertising copy, created newsletters, made up back cover content—in fact, I'd do just about anything to produce some income from my writing. I edited manuscripts, worked as a ghostwriter, created study guides, and worked with pastors to turn their sermon series into books. Eventually that figure jumped to $300 per month. Then $500. Then $1000 per month. When I set a goal of making $1500 per month, that's when I figured I was going to become a full-time writer.

MacGregor is realistic about others following this advice. "That said, there's nothing in Scripture that says you are necessarily called to follow that same path. As I said earlier, publishing a book doesn't validate your life. Perhaps God is calling you to write to your local church or to your family. Perhaps the words you write are only for you. There's value in writing, not just in getting published. So don't assume you must try to move toward writing as a full-time career. Many of the authors I now represent have other jobs, activities, and sources of income—that doesn't keep them from making an impact on the world through their writing."

We are not advising readers of this book to do any-thing other than carefully consider where they are finan-cially now and where they want to be in the future. We are not saying, "Quit your job and jump into full-time writing." That may work for some but not for all. One person who did leave one career to enter full-time writing is Vicki Caruana. Consider her story about how this happened. "People say that it is difficult to make a living as a writer. A writer writes, always. As a full-time writer, I write many different things in order to pay the bills. I write articles, books, Internet copy, and curriculum, and I teach writing classes. But it didn't start that way. I left a full-time teaching job to become a full-time freelance writer. It was a risk. And there's lots of advice out there as to when to take the plunge. Beginning writers do not get the highest pay, so write a lot! If this is what you're called to do, you'll do it regardless of the pay. But you must also be a good steward of your time and the responsibilities you have."

Another full-timer is Ken Walker. When asked about the matter of making a living and what he would tell beginners, Walker urged caution.

> It will take a long time to establish yourself, so
> don't jump off the cliff and find your heart
> stopping because you no longer have a steady
> income. I would advise anyone who wants to
> write to decide first what kind of writing you
> want to do, how you can do it, and when you can
> do it. If you have two young children at home, it
> may not be the best time to start unless you can
> find time at eleven o'clock at night or five o'clock
> in the morning.

Also, realize that many publications don't pay that well yet may be great places to break in. The first task is to collect some bylines so your experience opens doors with larger magazines. Although I generally don't believe in writing for free, even that may be a way to get off the ground (just don't make a habit of it). The point, though, is to work your way up to better and better paying markets. Recognize, too, that some secular markets pay much better than Christian, and you may want to write for some of them to help provide more income for your Christian work. I focus most of my writing on Christian markets and stay busy with it, but there is no sin in writing for secular publications. Also, developing reprint markets and spinning off other stories from assignments will provide additional income for minimal amounts of time.

Kathi Macias has valuable advice here. "Keep your day job! That many seem an obvious answer, but far too many aspiring writers go into this profession with their eyes wide shut. They hear of the one writer who made it big with a first novel and think they will do the same. That's a little like hearing about the guy who won the lottery and assuming you can buy a ticket and retire from the proceeds. It simply isn't realistic. I started out writing for free in order to build my resume. My first published article paid $25, but that was alright, because it encouraged me to keep going and not give up."

We have all heard of people who make large incomes from writing, but those are the rare exceptions. Cecil

Murphey offers a helpful perspective on this issue. "Forget the money. If money is a big issue, writing probably isn't the way to go. I started by writing articles for Christian periodicals. I knew I wouldn't make a living that way, and it didn't matter. I simply wanted to write. We estimate that only 2 percent of writers make a living at writing. Most of them support themselves by speaking, teaching, editing, or other jobs. In the Christian marketplace, I know of two ways to make a living exclusively as a writer. We can write one or two best sellers, or we can write prolifically. I've had a few best sellers (books I've ghostwritten that still bring in royalties), but I also write two or three books a year."

The consensus here is simple—write because you want to write, not because you want to make a lot of money.

7. What do you think of the editorial task?

Both of us—Don and Len—have served as editors at various stages of our careers. Len is a full-time editor now, and Don spent over two years as the editor of special projects for a missions organization and has edited several books as a freelance writer. We wanted to get the perspectives of the writers we interviewed on the editing task. What do they think of editors? How do they work with editors? What have their experiences been?

Everyone has heard horror stories of writers who work on a project and turn in what they consider a masterpiece, only to have it butchered by some frustrated editor. On the other side, editors tell stories about arrogant writers who will not listen to reasonable advice. Which side is right?

They both are! Those things do happen on occasion, but there is a safe middle ground. Learn to think of an editor as an ally in the long process of having a work published.

Cecil Murphey has what we believe is a good attitude toward this issue. "Everybody needs an editor. We never reach the place where someone can't make our work better. Long ago I decided that books and articles are products. Editors want me to look good, and the finished product makes editors look good. The best part is that readers will never know how much help we received from editors. They'll think we're better writers than we are."

Stephen Clark tells writers, "A good editor will work with a writer to make the writer look his or her best. I need and depend on good editors. Working with a talented editor is a delight. Working with a bad editor is a nightmare!" Vicki Caruana is definitely in the editors' corner. "I believe that it is my responsibility as a writer to provide an editor with as clean a manuscript as possible—that is, free from error. I spend a lot of time revising before he or she ever sees it. Once I am working with my editor, it is usually a good experience if we both have the same vision for the book/article. If not, it can be a tug-of-war. A good editor is worth his weight in gold, in my opinion."

Alan Maki recognizes the value of proficient editors. "The editorial task is part of the game, and I accept it. I realize that my editors have much expertise, and I have learned much from these experts. I don't believe in bucking their advice but accepting it and 'going with the flow.' I don't believe in protecting every word I write but understand that rewriting and reshaping is necessary and will make the thoughts and ideas even better. If one does not accept or embrace the editorial task, get out of writing. If you think you know it all, you don't."

Jan Coleman works as an editor for a writers' service. Her perspective is helpful. "I edit manuscripts for a critique service. While my weakness is details, dotting i's and crossing t's, I have an eye for seeing where to improve the manuscript—others', of course, as it's tough to spot the flaws in our own." That aspect of the objective view is important. When a writer is too close to the work, seeing it with an objective eye is all but impossible. Susan Titus Osborn, too, serves writers by working as a freelance editor. Regarding editing, she contends, "That is the most important phase of writing, and editors want clean copy sent to them. Helping others to edit their work and editing it for them provide my bread-and-butter money."

The rule of thumb for the writer-editor relationship according to Chip MacGregor is simple—trust. "Trust your editor. Simple as that. Don't haggle, don't argue, don't insist on always being right. A fresh set of eyes looking at your material is one of the best ways to improve your work. Most of the writers I meet are amateurs. Most of the working editors I meet are professionals. Trust your editor. Your editor will be wrong, of course. The writing you're doing is undoubtedly far beyond his or her ability to grasp. But humor everyone and go along with it. Trust your editor."

Ted Baehr sums up nicely the issue of editors and their work: "I love editing and editors. Editors make the writer much better."

8. Since good writers are always wide readers, what two or three books have you read recently you could recommend to other writers?

Occasionally, as we travel around the country speaking at writers' conferences, people will casually say to us, "Well, I really don't have time to read since I'm busy writing." We want to say to those people that they need to expand their horizons and perspectives. If you never read anything, then you're writing will be pretty thin soup.

When we asked the working writers for this book what they were reading, we got what we expected—a wide variety of books from many genres. These writers know that they need to stoke the fires of their own minds in order to have anything valuable to say. Here are some of the books that have recently made an impact on some of the writers who participated in this chapter.

Chip MacGregor offers titles specifically on writing. "*In the Beginning* by Alister McGrath. Every writer should know about the invention of movable type and the genesis of our industry. *Dickens' Fur Coat and Charlotte's Unanswered Letters* by Daniel Pool. A fascinating look at how publishing moved from the realm of the wealthy and powerful to the street corners and into the homes of everyday working people. *The First Five Pages* by Noah Lukeman. An agent helps beginning writers see how significantly to improve your writing—and your odds for getting published."

For Jan Coleman, some of the recent helpful books include the following. "*Windows of the Soul* by Ken Gire.

It's not about writing but will inspire all writers. And *Snoopy's Guide to the Writing Life* by Monte Schulz, son of Charles Schulz, the cartoon strip's author. Every writer can relate to Snoopy, the canine would-be author, banging out stories on his manual typewriter atop his famous doghouse. Extras are thirty-two essays from best-selling writers about the joys and realities of the writing life. The book is perched on my bookcase, and I grab it when I'm frustrated and need a good chuckle."

Rather than giving specific titles or authors, Alan Maki gives his perspective on the need to keep reading. "As a pastor, I read a lot of Christian books and magazines. Rather than recommend specific books, as many will do, I say, 'Just read, read, read. Study, study, study. Compare, compare, compare. Devour, devour, devour. See how John Doe wrote it. Think how you would do it. There are many good books and writers.'"

Stephen Clark recommends specific authors rather than titles. "First, I'd recommend, rather than titles, a few authors. Read Tom Wolfe, Anna Quindlen, Tracy Kidder, Peggy Noonan, and others. I love James Dickey, John Updike, and John Cheever. On the Christian side, Francis Schaeffer, Phil Yancey, and C. S. Lewis are great. Don't let yourself get stuck reading only one author or one genre. Read wide and deep, and tackle some of the deeper stuff. And read a wide range of magazines as well, like *Christianity Today, Discipleship Journal, World, Time, Newsweek,* etc."

Susan Titus Osborn makes a good point about not getting stuck in one genre of reading or writing. "I think it is important to read outside your genre. I mostly write nonfiction, but I read fiction and am one of the Christy judges. The latest good fiction I have read includes

Beyond the Sacred Page by Jack Cavanaugh, *Fire by Night* by Lynn Austin, and *First Light* by Bodie and Brock Thoene—all Christy winners."

Ted Baehr offers the following as recent favorites: *A Matter of Principle* by David Manuel; *Following Gandalf* by Matthew T. Dickerson; and *From Tabloid to Truth,* Dan Wooding's autobiography.

Vicki Caruana says her recent reading included these titles: Stephen King, *On Writing*; also, *The Forest for the Trees* and *Bird by Bird*. For fiction, *Peace like a River.* For nonfiction, *Why?* by Anne Graham Lotz.

Marvin Olasky recently enjoyed these: Shelby Foote, *The Civil War* and Whittaker Chambers, *Witness*.

For Ken Walker, the matter of reading is not just about a few favorite authors. It is about life itself. He says:

> Despite its obvious theological flaws, *Tuesdays with Morrie* is a delightful book. While it doesn't have much to do with writing, the author is a sports columnist whose life was consumed with work until he was reunited with his old college professor and learned that personal connections have more value than making money. I liked it because, as a writer, I tend to get wrapped up in work, earning enough money to pay our bills and hoping for a best seller (or at least enough sales to generate some book royalties). But this book reminded me that being a decent person and investing time in relationships are as important as a byline.
>
> I also just picked up a book at a writers conference by Dennis Hensley titled *Money Wise,*

which goes into basic financial management and investing. Writers tend to be creative and naïve, as if God will drop everything into our lap. We need reminders that God expects us to be wise stewards of our money and develop more sense about handling what he provides.

Finally, while I'm not a novelist, I love reading novels. *Breach of Promise* by James Scott Bell is one of the best recent releases on the market, along with Ted Dekker's new trilogy. (Anything Dekker writes is great, in case you haven't discovered him.) Another of my favorite authors is T. Davis Bunn. Read *The Great Divide* and *Drummer in the Dark.* Masterpieces.

Like other writers, Kathi Macias has her favorite authors. She notes, "My very favorite fiction authors are Bodie and Brock Thoene. Anyone aspiring to write good fiction should not only read the Thoenes' work for enjoyment, but also to learn the craft. Among my favorite nonfiction authors are Max Lucado and Brennan Manning. They say so much, and yet they say it so succinctly and so beautifully. Their words sing! Any of their words are profitable reads."

Cecil Murphey also demonstrates the value of wide reading.

I recently read Heather Gemmen's powerful memoir, *Startling Beauty* (Cook Communications, 2004). That's the kind of honesty we need to see more of in Christian publishing. It's a powerful story, and it's the best writing I've seen in CBA. I also read *Not Fade Away: A Short Life Well Lived* by Laurence Shames and Peter Barton

(Rodale Press, 2003). This book is about Peter Barton, an outstanding businessman, who died of stomach cancer. In his dying months he and Shames wrote this as a book of hope.

In fiction I've recently finished Michael Connelly's *The Narrows* (Little, Brown, 2004). I've read all fourteen books that Connelly has written (and in chronological order). I like his style, his characters, and his plots.

There is an obvious lesson here. One who would write for others should also learn to love the written word in its broadest context. After all, Christ came as "the Word" (John 1:1).

9. Anything else you would like to say to would-be writers?

After we asked our interviewees specific questions about the writing life and process, we asked an open-ended question in case they would like to say something else to beginning writers. As with all their other responses, these women and men have offered their hard-learned advice about this most subtle of crafts.

Alan Maki says, "If you love to write and you know you're good, then write! But remember, you need to understand all you can about the process of getting published, and you must do the hard work, which is rewriting and rewriting some more. You can take that advice to the bank!" (He should know because he takes it to the bank himself.)

Chip MacGregor offers hope to any writer who may be struggling with self-doubt and anxiety. "It's nice to have talent. Training is great, but having genuine talent is a rare treat. I've yet to meet a wonderfully talented writer who nobody wants to publish."

Jan Coleman reminds people that writing is a gift that must be satisfied and cannot be denied. "If you're a born writer, you can't *not* write. It's in your blood. Whether you get paid or not, whether you get an audience or not. My best advice is this: try everything writing has to offer. Submit, submit, submit, and don't consider rejection as failure. Persistence is your strongest asset."

Coleman continues, "Don't set your sights on mainstream books and give up if you don't make it. Not all born writers are meant to know fame or even publish a book. Shoot for the moon, but adjust your expectations as you see where your niche is. Maybe it's using your skills to compile others' memoirs. I see a big need for that, and many older people who don't want their stories to die with them are willing to pay for it." She also urges writers to study the markets to understand what is happening in the larger world of publishing. "Keep up on the market. I can't tell you how many writers I talk to who don't recognize best-selling authors' names. They have no idea what are the hot trends in publishing or top publishing houses. Most of my would-be-author friends aren't interested enough, and that's one of the reasons they're not published. With the Internet, keeping up with what's going on in your area of writing interest is not that difficult."

Stephen Clark reminds everyone, both beginners and veterans, to keep the spiritual focus alive. "Don't get caught up in writing just for money or profit. Don't think more highly of yourself just because you're a published writer. Don't compromise your ethics or beliefs. Don't write something you don't believe just to get a paycheck. In all you do and write, honor God, exalt Christ, be inspired by the Holy Spirit, and study to make sure that every word aligns with God's Word."

Vicki Caruana recognizes that the written word, to be effective, must be treated with excellence. She contends, "Some writers write because their writing is a means to an end. Maybe they are looking for fame or to become a personality of sorts. Others write because they must, and the writing itself is the end they seek. Either way, write with excellence. It's the only way to do it."

Kathi Macias urges writers to remember why they began writing in the first place. "If you believe this is what God has called and gifted you to do, don't give up; at the same time, don't settle for mediocre work under the guise that your work is inspired by God and therefore doesn't need improvement. Remember the admonition in Habakkuk: 'Write the vision . . .and make it plain.' This is the verse that is the basis for all the writing classes I teach. I believe that good writing is a two-part process: first, getting the vision down on paper and second, rewriting and editing the piece until it is clear and concise, and the very best it can be."

Full-time freelancer Ken Walker has thought much about the writing life and its challenges. He advises, "If God called you to write, you will find a way. I know two seminary professors who have written books despite full-time teaching loads and pastoring churches part-time. I asked one when he wrote his latest novel, and he said, 'By writing from 6 to 8 a.m., six days a week.' The other said he wrote one of his books over several months between 11 p.m. and 2 a.m., after the kids had gone to bed. So, you see, you do have the time if you make the time.

"The big drawback I see with so many would-be writers is they aren't really serious about it. They allow television, family obligations, shopping, and a million other distractions to sidetrack them. In addition, too many would-be writers like to daydream about writing but aren't willing to invest the time and effort it takes to be a writer. Or they just want to dabble in it. It's fine if you want to make it a hobby, but don't waste people's time acting as if you want to write unless you're serious about it."

Cecil Murphey sums up his view of writing this way: "Keep learning; don't give up. I believe anyone who continually seeks to get better and stays at the craft can make it as a writer."

We end this chapter with a writers' creed offered by Susan Titus Osborn. It's a great reminder to take it in, then hand it on.

Writers' Creed

When you are learning, seek help.

When you are published, pass it on.

CHAPTER 5
Writing: From the Editors' Perspective

Throughout this book we have stressed the importance of doing your homework and research into both your subject matter and the publishing process. Some writers say, "I love to write, but I can't stand the business stuff. I'll just leave that up to the publishing house." That is an understandable sentiment but a misguided one. As a writer seeking publication, you are responsible for everything regarding your work, from the initial idea through the printing process culminating in helping to sell the book. Thus, the more you know about the entire process, the better off you will be.

One important piece of the publishing puzzle is to understand what makes editors tick. Why do they make the decisions they make? What factors cause them to reject some manuscripts and accept others? What mistakes do they see writers make over and over? In order to help answer these and other important questions, we asked a number of editors to talk frankly about the entire scope of Christian writing today. They responded enthusiastically and gave us the information you will read in this chapter.

We asked several questions that the editors represented here answered. If you study their replies and take to heart their advice, you will be light-years ahead of the person who does not know this information. Remember, no one will do your work for you. Getting your foot into the editorial door can sometimes result in bruises, but all wounds heal! Learn from the editors and then go on and slide your shoe right in there.

Directions from Christian Editors

Imagine yourself sitting down with a group of editors over coffee and saying to them, "OK, be honest. Tell me frankly what you know that will help me succeed as a writer." In a sense that is what this section does. A group of editors "takes the gloves off" and tells it straight.

1. What can you, as an editor, tell beginning writers that will help them succeed?

To this general question Andrew T. LePeau, editorial director of InterVarsity Press, gave this life-perspective answer: "Be sure you have life credentials for what you're writing. Be involved in ministry and in people's lives. Be knowledgeable on your subject, widely read. Be aware of the market and similar books."

By "life credentials" LePeau means that you actually live what you are writing. This does not mean that you must have a Ph.D. in your subject but that you have enough experience to say something important. Personal experiences can be great teachers, as many who have earned graduate degrees at the university of hard knocks can attest.

Gary Terashita, former editor at Broadman & Holman and now with Warner Faith, points out that two things will help beginners. "Because I deal with intrinsically Christian books that are to do the work of the ministry, the first thing I tell writers is to be sure that writing for the public is something God wants from them. Next, because Christian writing should be glorifying to him, it should be of the highest quality. The importance of the message is diminished by poor writing." Terashita advises that writers pursue three basics in this regard: read the best available in the chosen genre; read and study books on the craft of writing; and practice to hone talent.

Ted Griffin, senior editor of Crossway Books, sees many writers, especially beginners, trying to get by without the hard work involved in perfecting the art of writing. "Go for the highest quality possible in your research and writing. Don't cut corners. Don't settle for so-so results. And always keep your specific readership in mind—what will reach them, touch them, communicate with them?"

Terry Whalin is an acquisitions editor for Howard Publishing Company. He actually wears hats of both freelance writer and editor. Whalin notes that beginning writers need to realize that while Christian publishing is a ministry, the financial aspects of the business cannot be overlooked. Many people have input into the decision to publish a book. Whalin calls this a "consensus-building process." He says, "I may be convinced your book project is perfect for our needs, but I have to convince a number of other people including my fellow editors, sales people, marketing personnel, and the leaders of the publishing house your book is worthy to appear in print. For any publisher to take your book and print it, they will spend about $25,000 to $35,000, and this cost includes only a modest advance to the author ($5,000 or less)." Beginning writers who have an awareness of this side of the business could avoid feeling ignored or rejected if their projects are not up to the standards of currently published writers. Someone has to pay for the publishing, and the company needs to know that a financial expenditure will generate enough revenue to keep them in business.

2. What mistakes do you see beginners making over and over?

The editors who responded to our questions have many decades of combined experience. All have noticed some of the same mistakes that beginning writers make. Their advice will help you avoid them.

Ted Griffin says, "They try to reach too broad a readership. They are careless and don't edit their own work carefully enough, missing obvious typos, awkward sentence structure, etc. And, most important, they are sloppy in their theology or doctrinal articulation, failing to remember that being true to the Word of God is crucial."

Gary Terashita knows how important precision and accuracy are to a writer. Many beginners forget this fact. He says, "Beginners most often think that they should just put to paper what comes to mind. This results in meandering, poorly constructed and worded work. These almost always contain clichés, simple or boring language, and scatter-gun thoughts that do not hold a reader's interest. It is also obvious that once the stream of consciousness is in print, it is immediately stuffed in a folder to be offered for review." Terashita knows that writing the initial draft is only the first step of a long process to produce a worthy manuscript. "I believe that the best work in writing is done in the rewrites."

Terry Whalin sees beginning nonfiction writers working on their manuscripts without a clear vision of what is necessary to have it published.

> About 90 percent of nonfiction books are contracted from a book proposal. If you are writing a nonfiction manuscript, then you are wasting your time. The proposal contains information about you, the market, and the competition for your idea which would not be in a book manuscript. You need to work hard on your book proposal to show you're keenly aware of the market. Visualize your book. How long will it be? Where will it appear in a bookstore? What books will be beside it (your competition)? Don't tell me that you will not have any competition and your idea is unique. It is not true. Your book will compete with something else and is not totally unique. Publishers are jaded and roll their eyes at this common statement from new writers. What are you going to do to market and push your book into new areas for sales? This type of information has to be built into your proposal and will help it stand out from the others on the editor's desk.

One mistake Andy LePeau sees in beginners is what he calls The First Book Syndrome. He describes it this way: "Writers think they've got to put everything they ever thought about anything in their book. They don't realize they can write more than one book. Often just taking a piece of a book idea is best. A book about everything is a book about nothing.

"Similarly, writers often try to do too much. That is, they think they can reach two audiences at once—for

example, trying to reach those who are hooked on cigarettes *and* those who love those hooked on cigarettes.
Better to write the book for one audience or the other and
let the second audience read over the shoulders of the first.
By trying to reach two audiences, writers end up missing
both audiences. A book for everyone is a book for no one."

3. How realistic in today's publishing environment is a beginning writer's chances of being published?

One thing most beginning writers want to know is
this—can they really get published? Is it possible for a
novice to see his book in print or her project bound and
on bookstore shelves? The answer from these experienced editors is a cautious yes. "Cautious" because every
writer, especially beginning unknowns, simply must take
account of the competition their project will face. Only a
finite number of books can be published and absorbed
into the marketplace. With that fact in mind, our editors
give their take on this issue.

Ted Griffin gives a realistic assessment. He says, "It is
becoming increasingly difficult for a new writer to get
published by an established, traditional publisher.
Publishers are becoming more picky about what they will
publish, some even refusing to consider any truly unsolicited manuscripts. And even literary agents are becoming more particular about who they will represent. Thus,
high quality is more important than ever."

The last statement about high quality is one every
reader of this book should underscore, highlight, and
memorize. You *can* make it with a commitment to excellence and hard work.

But the question remains: is it realistic to seek publication? One well-known editor gives the odds at roughly one in one hundred. Only about one project out of one hundred will make it to publication. That may sound discouraging, but it is the reality. Thus, reading books like this one and others about writing and publishing will give you a head start over would-be authors who will not do the hard work of learning everything possible about the process.

When Andy LePeau considers this question, he realizes there are two parts of Christian publishing—the academic and the general.

"For academic publishing, it is less of a problem. Authors automatically come with credentials of advanced degrees or prominent teaching positions. Academic audiences are less concerned (but not entirely unconcerned) with who wrote it and more concerned with content. If it's really good, it can get published.

"For general publishing, platform is essential—a mailing list, an organization to help promote the book, well-known people who will offer endorsements, a regular speaking schedule—whatever the author can bring to the table is a must. Beginning authors (and some published authors) think that publishers can magically sell tens of thousands of copies. Publishers do have some systems that can help, but they can't do it alone. An author should be able to sell as many as a publisher."

This last statement will surprise many new writers. They think, *What? The publisher expects me to help sell the book! That's their job.* The fact is it is everybody's job. The more writers are willing to help market their books, the better chances they have of landing a publishing offer.

4. Do you have any wisdom regarding techniques for a writer wanting to move from idea to manuscript?

OK, so you have a great idea for a book. Now what? How can you go from idea to manuscript? What should you keep in mind here? Gary Terashita points out that a writer must do the hard work of researching the topic to ensure that the subject matter will have a wide appeal. Just because your mother likes the idea does not mean that it is a publishable concept. He says, "Comments from a few friends and family members are not a basis upon which publishing decisions are made."

Techniques that move an idea from concept to publication include having a laser-like sharpness for the project, according to Ted Griffin. "Key points here include doing a developed outline for the proposed book, drafting a concise but complete mission statement for the work, and specifically identifying the intended readership. Many writers want to skip these steps, but their book will then fail on crucial points."

5. How do you define the task of editing?

An understanding of what editors do will help writers grasp the work that goes on behind the scenes to make a successful book. Some of the editors we surveyed for this book shed some light on their work.

So how do editors define their jobs? Andy LePeau sums it up in one word—coaching. For him, the task of editing is this: "Being an honest friend. Taking something good and making it better." Writers should expect the editor to bring his or her expertise to the table and offer it in order to make the manuscript better. We have all heard of editors who receive letters with manuscripts that say, "This manuscript is perfect. It was inspired by God, so do not change one word when you publish it." Do you really think it might get published?

Ted Griffin agrees that editors work hard at helping writers produce a better finished product. He defines editing, "Quality control—polishing—helping the author communicate clearly and effectively—being a middle-man between author and publisher." Gary Terashita also agrees that the editorial task is to help the writer improve. "Substantive editing should help the author further sharpen the message and refine the overall quality of the manuscript without doing violence to the author's voice."

6. What do editors do? Briefly describe your work.

When asked to define his work, one editor responded simply, "Read manuscripts. Say no to a lot of manuscripts. Work a lot with sales and marketing. Travel. Answer a lot of e-mail." That is a good thumbnail description, but, of course, the work of editing is more involved than this simple summary might suggest. Gary Terashita notes that many editors wear two hats. One is the acquiring of man-uscripts from authors (thus the title, acquisitions editor). The other hat involves actually working through the man-uscript word by word to make it readable and grammati-cally correct.

Terashita says, "I am an acquisitions editor, so most of my job is finding and signing authors and projects. I manage the process of adding books to our list from ini-tial contact through contract and manuscript delivery and approval. The remainder of my job requires my substantive editorial work on the manuscript to ensure a book that fulfills the contract and fits our ministry goals."

Ted Griffin describes his day-to-day work this way: "I work my way through a manuscript, catching typos, awkward sentences, theological errors or fuzziness, inconsistencies in style or details of content, checking the accuracy of Scripture quotations and other quoted materials where possible, etc."

7. Can you say something about developing the editor-author relationship?

Editors dedicate their lives to taking the products of writers and honing and polishing each one so that it becomes the best possible work. Everyone has heard of the battles between egotistical writers and stubborn editors, but these are—or should be—rare. Your authors of this book, Don and Len, wrote this book with the hope that writers with something vital to say will learn to develop a professional attitude toward the entire publishing process. Part of this process involves learning to work with editors. Contrary to some popular opinions, editors are not fire-breathing dragons just waiting to incinerate your manuscript and send back the ashes! (Well, most of them aren't.) They are people who are using their gifts and abilities to serve God by publishing the best possible books. They are not your enemies. They are your allies in striking a blow for the kingdom of God.

Editors generally like developing personal relationships with authors. Some of those relationships last for years. For example, we—Don and Len—started working together in the early 1980s when we cowrote a book for a company that does not even exist today. We have worked on many other projects together over the years, including several that we cowrote, one that we coedited, and two that Don wrote and Len edited. Over the years we have spoken at events together all over the country and have visited each other's homes. Once we even spent a thoroughly weird day visiting Graceland in Memphis on Elvis's birthday! The point is that writers and editors can develop strong working relationships. Doing so takes effort and openness on both parties. You cannot count on your editor becoming your close friend, but you probably can anticipate his or her desire to work closely on the project to make it the best possible finished product.

We will discuss the role of agents later in this book. One of the results of agents getting involved in Christian publishing is that the author-editor relationship has changed. Sometimes the author hardly gets to know the editor at all because the agent is a go-between in the process. Even so, the editors who gave us their expertise for this book understand that the writer and the editor are a team.

Ted Griffin observes, "This must be a team mentality; they must not be rivals or competitors in any sense. They are partners in the publishing process, though the editor must remember that the book is primarily the author's, and he must not edit so heavily or so insensitively that the book ends up not fully representing what the author is trying to say. A friendship and mutual respect between the author and editor is desirable and needed."

For Gary Terashita, this issue involves a fine balancing act. "The essence of this for me is remembering that I am working with my brothers and sisters in Christ and that Scripture calls me to a high standard in these relationships.

The trick can be in balancing the needs and interests of the author with those of the publishing house."

Because an editor has probably worked on many more books than an author has, he or she will have more expertise to offer about the process of getting the manuscript ready for publication. Andy LePeau says this can work in authors' favor if they are willing to heed the advice. "Authors obviously have something to bring to the table. And editors don't know everything. But most editors have published dozens or even hundreds of books, and most authors have published only a few. So the relative experience differential means authors should take seriously what editors say."

LePeau, too, sees this relationship as something to which both parties contribute. "I think of it as a partnership. Neither has control. Both can have veto power. It's a case of mutual submission, I think. Authors who have strong opinions, require things to go their way, are authors we don't do a second book with." What is needed is some humility on the part of the author. LePeau points out that the leadership book, *Good to Great* by Jim Collins describes levels of influence in leaders. LePeau says the author of that book affirms Level-5 Leaders—those who combine great passion for the organization with great personal humility. He says, "We look for Level-5 authors— those who combine great passion for their message and content with great personal humility."

You may be wondering how you can actually get to know an editor. One of the best ways is to attend a writers conference where editors are present and meet them in person. Dozens of conferences are held in various locations each year. Many of them have editors who lead workshops and meet writers. They are open to listening to article or book ideas.

Terry Whalin says this is an excellent way to meet editors, and it will prevent writers from making some blunders. "Conferences are great for these relationship-building experiences. Don't try to do it on the phone (you will waste the editor's time—from their perspective). It's a huge mistake for you to call the publishing house and ask the editor how to submit your materials. You are not building a relationship. Instead you are showing your lack of professional courtesy and building a negative memory with this particular editor because from his or her perspective you are wasting time that should be spent elsewhere."

Information on conferences is given in chapter 10 of this book.

8. How do you want to be approached by writers—queries, proposals, manuscripts? Hard copy? E-mail?

OK, you have a great idea for a book. Now reality sets in—how do you actually get it to an editor if you have not met that person? This is a more important issue than some beginning writers realize. As the gatekeeper, an editor is the first line of contact between author and publisher. There never was a time when an author could just stop by a publisher's office and ask to visit with an editor. While that may have happened on rare occasions, the more prevalent experience was for the author to contact the editor, usually by mail, and ask to submit the work.

The publishing industry in general, and the Christian publishing industry in particular, is changing. Many book publishers are closing the editorial door on freelance writers. Some will not accept an unsolicited proposal, much less a full manuscript. This is why we urge writers to check the guidelines for a potential publisher. Most will have submission guidelines on their Web sites. Sally E. Stuart's annual book, *Christian Writers' Market Guide,* also has lists of publishers and their preferred ways to be contacted. Each is different. When writers contact them in ways that are not appropriate, the editor reads "amateur" all over the contact. That is not a way to endear yourself to an editor. Usually, all you get is a rejection slip.

The small number of editors we surveyed for this book bear out the reality that every publisher is unique. For example, when Andy LePeau at InterVarsity Press (IVP) was asked which method he prefers—queries, proposals, manuscripts, hard copy, e-mail—his reply was simply, "Actually, any of the above is fine." On the other hand, Ted Griffin has a completely different approach. He says, "At this time, Crossway Books is accepting proposals only from established authors or through agents. We are accepting no unsolicited manuscripts." Gary Terashita at Warner Faith wants writers to read their guidelines, prepare a proposal in Word, and attach it to an e-mail.

A serious freelance writer will study the publishers' guidelines carefully and then follow them. That will save many wasted hours of effort on parts of both writer and publisher.

9. What do you look for in a good proposal?

A book proposal is a summary of the content of the book. The next chapter of this book has more about this, but for now consider what our group of editors advise. Generally, proposals are used for nonfiction books and contain several key elements. Andy LePeau gives a good description of what a proposal should contain.

A proposal should include:

First, a cover letter that includes:

1. *A concept statement.* In fifty to one hundred words, summarize the main problem or issue the book will address, the subject and scope of the book, the audience, and what benefits it will offer readers.

2. *The passion for the book.* Tell why you are passionate about the idea for your book, why your message is important, and how it will make a difference.

3. *Who the book is for.* Explain who the audience is, how you know these people, and why your book will communicate effectively to them.

4. *The length of the book.* Estimate how many typewritten, double-spaced pages it will be or its projected word count.

5. *Time line.* When the draft of the manuscript will be complete.

6. *A review of competing/similar books.* What recent books are most similar to yours? List title, author, publisher, price, length for each. Briefly explain how your book is different.

7. *Credentials.* Your background, education, experience that contribute toward your writing the book.

The second major component of the proposal is a chapter-by-chapter summary. Outlines are not helpful because they list only the topics to be covered and not what the author intends to say about those topics. Instead, provide one or two paragraphs summarizing each chapter. A couple of sample chapters or writing samples at the same level and style and for the same audience would also be helpful.

Ted Griffin notes that a writer should work hard on the cover letter and the proposal. Otherwise, "If the cover letter is poorly written, why would we expect the book itself to be well written?" Good question! Gary Terashita also observes that good writing in the proposal indicates the possibility of good writing in the manuscript. He says, "Brevity and clarity. I also judge the writing of the entire proposal, not just the sample chapters. Most commonly missing are previous book publishing history with accurate sales numbers."

Terry Whalin agrees that writers of nonfiction should spend a great deal of time and energy on a book proposal. A proposal is a synopsis on the book, but it is also a sales letter. You are selling the idea to the editor. It should be complete and compelling. It should contain the best writing you are capable of producing. Whalin says, "Your proposal has to be written well and in the expected format. No graduation certificates are needed with your submission (yes, I've seen them). Skip the colored paper or weird fonts (yes, I've seen these as well). Leave out the fancy notebooks or costly presentation folders. These things get attention but mostly negative attention."

Writers should always include a self-addressed stamped envelope or instructions to discard the manuscript and respond with a single stamped envelope or include an e-mail address if the materials are rejected. Whalin shows why this is necessary.

Without the SASE, you have no hope of receiving a response from the publisher. Imagine receiving six to ten thousand unsolicited submissions in a year without any return postage. Imagine yourself in the role of the publishing house, and consider your choice—throw the manuscript or use money from your already tight budget to return them. It is not hard to determine that the publisher will toss your materials and never respond. You need to study the market (something you've heard), learn how to present marketing material and yourself to be unique with well-written material. It is not easy but possible. A typical excellent nonfiction book proposal is about fifteen to twenty pages—just for the proposal materials.

Whalin knows that writers who take the time and trouble to focus and sharpen the concept in a proposal stand a higher chance of publishing their book. "Your challenge (and goal) as a writer is to send an absolutely irresistible proposal to the publisher. If you follow these steps, then you will separate your materials from the many other manuscripts which arrive at the same time. It will help the acquisitions editor and also improve your possibilities to be one of the few proposals which become a book."

10. What categories do you publish?

Trying to decide which publisher to contact can seem like moving through a maze. How can you figure out which is best for your proposed project? Just as doing your homework on how publishers want to be contacted is important, so is zeroing in on certain publishers. Not every company publishes the same kind of material. Some only do nonfiction while others specialize in fiction. Some publish only writers from their denomination. For others, denominational affiliation is unimportant.

Your task is to do your homework in finding those markets that best suit what you are trying to accomplish. It is not enough to say, "I'll work with anybody willing to publish me!" That sentiment is understandable, but it is not realistic. Publishing houses are usually clear about what they do and whom they work with.

Ted Griffin at Crossway Books says his company publishes in the areas of contemporary issues, academic theological works, family, Christian living/applied theology, commentaries, and illustrated children's books. These latter books are all developed in-house.

IVP publishes in these areas according to Andy LePeau: academic, Bible study guides, reference, general trade books, especially on prayer, apologetics, spiritual formation, current issues, cultural critique, multiethnic issues, evangelism, and leadership.

These categories can be moving targets too. Companies often shift their emphases. This is another reason for writers to stay on top of trends and movements in publishing.

CHAPTER 6
Constructing the Book Proposal

What do you think a publisher wants to see when you are shopping manuscripts? You might imagine that most would actually want to see the finished manuscript, right? But this is not true. Almost no publisher wants to know that a writing project is finished before a publishing decision has been made and before they have had a chance to offer some input into the writing. Most editors want to be able to interact with the writer, to have a chance to shape the project early on in the writing and publishing process. In this way they can tailor the project to their company's publishing guidelines, make sure the material is directed to an identifiable reading audience, and be sure it covers what the intended market needs.

Since few publishing houses have a commitment anymore to review unsolicited materials, if you send them a finished or substantially finished manuscript, it will probably be returned to you without even being read.

Do Your Homework

What do publishers want to see? First, they want to see that you have done your homework. When you submit a manuscript or manuscript idea to an editor, you need to determine what category your book falls into. Many authors seem to have no idea about this when they are asked what category of book they are writing. They are working on a manuscript, or have even finished one, and apparently they have never thought about the category of their book! A book needs to *fit* somewhere in a bookstore, and books are shelved by *category*. Is your book biography or business? Is it church life or Christian living? Are you writing a novel? Which kind? There are different genres or categories of fiction, including classic, allegory, futuristic, historical, romance, Western, suspense, and contemporary. Are you writing a book for Christian education or biblical counseling? Is it about evangelism, family devotions, church history, or hermeneutics? You get the idea: the first thing you as an author must do is figure out just what it is you are doing, and this means categorizing your writing work.

Next you need to find helpful reference material in a good library that will help you locate publishers who publish the kinds of books you are writing. What kind of reference material can you find? There are periodically updated guides to the religious book markets that will be of help to you. For example, in most libraries of any size you can find volumes such as *The Writer's Market, Literary Market Place, Gebbe's Directory of Small Presses,* or *Herman's Guides to Editors, Literary Supplements, and Agents.* These volumes, and others like them, will show you what kinds of books a given publisher specializes in. They also list requirements for submission and will most likely include an address and phone number of the house—along with the names of the acquisition editors in many cases. Writers should study these books closely to determine which publishers they think would be interested in their writing projects. It is important for you to show you have done a thorough job of research on the publishing company *before* you contact them. (By the way, these guides will also give writers the names and locations of literary agents who work with Christian books as a specialty.)

You can also find in many bookstores some volumes that will give you the same kind of information on specifically *Christian* publishers. There is, for example, the *Christian Writers' Market Guide,* which is a reference tool for the Christian writer updated annually by Sally Stuart, who wrote the foreword to this book. With this kind of tool in hand, you will know what Zondervan, Tyndale House, or Broadman & Holman wants to publish. You will know not to send fiction to W Publishing and not to send anything to Thomas Nelson without an agent. If you are writing in the area of contemporary critical issues, there are publishing houses that might be interested in what you are doing because they publish books in this area. But because there are houses that do not publish books in this area, you need to know that too. Find out which house is which, and you do this by studying the market guides. The point is that you need to do your homework. If you don't show that you have done your research, your material will be returned to you in rapid fashion.

Don't Believe Everything You Read

What should you do after you have done your research? The first thing you should do is not believe everything you've just read! The reason for this is that publishing programs and personnel change on a regular basis, and the material in the guides can quickly become dated. Therefore, after you have consulted the guides, directly contact the publishers you consider appropriate—those houses that publish the kind of book you are writing and to whom you would like to submit your material. You can contact them by phone, e-mail, regular mail, or fax (the market guides will tell you how to contact them), and ask them to send you their author information and manuscript submission guidelines. Each publishing house that has any kind of an active publishing program will provide these guidelines for submission. Usually they are provided free of cost and are often available online at their Web sites.

These guidelines will explain the requirements for submission and what you should send along with your book proposal. Some editors want to see samples of your previous writing or samples from the actual manuscript you will be submitting. The guidelines will tell you what to send, so study them carefully for specific instructions as to submission requirements and any special slant that a publisher wants. For reasons that should be obvious, most editors at publishing houses want to see a query letter and a book proposal rather than an entire manuscript.

Getting Your Foot in the Editorial Door—the Query Letter

Now you are ready to send a query letter to the publisher or publishers you have carefully chosen. This letter will describe who you are, what your book is about, what makes it unique from any others like it already published and available in the marketplace, how it fits into the market, and why you feel it fits the company's needs. Usually this letter is sent before the actual book proposal. But some houses prefer you send it along with your book proposal or along with your manuscript or manuscript sample. Again, this depends on what the publisher wants to see, and you find this out by studying the market guides and the individual publisher's submission guidelines.

Because it is to your advantage to have your proposal evaluated by as many houses as are appropriate, there is nothing wrong with sending a query letter to more than one publisher at a time. The only caveat to this is being sure to let each house know that you are making simultaneous queries. A simultaneous submission of actual manuscripts is another thing entirely. A publisher does *not* want to invest money, time, and attention in the decision-making process only to find that other houses are looking at the same material and maybe have even made publishing offers.

Most houses want you to send a query letter only at first, and in this case the letter should be a business or sales letter describing your idea for a book and trying your best to convince the editor that this book deserves to be published. In the query letter, you are basically asking the editors whether they are interested in a book on a given topic that takes your special approach. In the final analysis, it will summarize the information you will cover in your book proposal, which we will talk about shortly, because while most houses do invite query letters regarding publishing a book, what they *really* want to see is a book proposal that details what the publishing project is all about, the structure it will take, the content that will be covered, the credentials of the author to write the book, a description of the target reading audience, and so on. Writing a good book proposal does two important things for you. First, it helps the editor better evaluate your book idea and see whether it fits with their publishing priorities. Second, it helps *you* clarify your own thinking about your book while you are involved in the actual research and writing process.

Keep in mind that your book proposal may be the only way you can get your foot in the editorial door at most publishing houses. It should be the best work you can do. Put it together, carefully, and make every word count. You've got to come across well. Your proposal has to be clear, direct, neatly produced, and organized. No typos! All the names, facts, and figures—everything—should be correct because this may be your one and only chance. Writing a book proposal is difficult, requiring an investment of time and attention. But make no mistake, with a well-done book proposal, your chances of getting published are much improved.

The Book Proposal

Before we suggest how to construct a good book proposal, let's ask what to include in one. The answer is, at least three things. First, sufficient information on the book's content. Second, your best guess at the market for the book—in other words, the intended reading audience for the book. And third, you need to include your biographical background and qualifications to write the proposed book. How long should your proposal be? It should be long enough to cover the pertinent information in sufficient detail but usually not longer than six pages. What form should the proposal take? Let's create an example of one now.

Let's pretend you are writing a nonfiction book, or you want to write one, about chicken plucking. In fact, you are a member of a small but proud breed of cotton-pickin' chicken pluckers. You are well aware that many Christians want to know about chicken plucking, but few books have been written on the subject, and most of the ones that have been written are long out of print. You want to write one that will inform and inspire, maybe a controversial one that will blow the top off the whole field of chicken plucking. Your book will be a real help to the church, especially at picnic times, and many will want to read it. Since you want to communicate with publishers to see if they have any interest in publishing a book on chicken plucking, what is the first thing you should do? The first thing to do is to prepare a book proposal that describes the book's content and market.

Get a Tentative Title

To determine the book's content, many writers say it always helps to come up with a working title before you've done anything else. Most publishers take a perverse glee in changing the author's suggested title, and many authors themselves revise their titles, so at this point this is just a working title to help you focus your thinking as you develop your book concept and proposal. Any ideas for this book? Is it for average Christians? How about *A Christian*

Guide to Cotton-Pickin' Chicken Plucking. Or maybe it's going to be a textbook to be used in a classroom situation. In that case, we could call it *Chicken Plucking Today: An Exposition of Contemporary Revisionist Chicken Plucking.* Whatever title you choose is at this point only a tentative one, but it is important because it will help you either summarize your thesis in the book or give the book's basic concept or premise. Instead of summarizing the book's content, sometimes a good title will hold out some hope or promise to the reader.

Content and Premise

After you have chosen a working title, then you can begin to consider what content the book will include. To do this, you must come up with a *premise.* The premise is a brief statement on the book's main idea that identifies the need for it in the marketplace and furthermore tells readers (in this case, your readers are the editors at the publishing house) what the book will describe or do for them. Our premise for *Chicken Plucking Today* could be something like this:

"*Chicken Plucking Today* will be a sixty-thousand-word book that includes the major presuppositions and expressions of what is variously called modernist, liberal, progressivist, revisionist, and experientialist chicken plucking and shows how some of the tentacles of liberal chicken plucking have found their way into evangelical chicken plucking."

That should do it. Have we addressed a need in this premise? Have we brought clarity and focus to the book concept? Yes, we told the editor or publishing panel what the book is going to cover, and we even proposed to show

how liberal chicken-plucking notions have found their way into evangelical chicken-plucking circles apparently without many of us even realizing what has happened. *Chicken Plucking Today* will sound the alert. We have stated a problem that we have identified in our premise. Coming up with a good premise is one of the most difficult things about writing an effective book proposal.

The Outline

Now that we have our book's premise, we must develop an outline to give both the author and the editor a clear sense of what is going to happen in the book and what is going to be covered. The outline needs to include section titles, chapter titles, and a sentence or two of description under each chapter title to show what will be covered in that chapter. Remember that at this point you are just making a start; the structure of the book and the approach in any of the given chapters can evolve over time— and probably they will be changed as you get deeper and deeper into it before the manuscript is finished.

As we think about our book on chicken plucking, we need to ask what should be the major sections or chapters. Maybe it could look something like this:

Introduction.

Chapter 1: Liberal Chicken Plucking Is Not New. Actually, chicken plucking today is done much the same way that it has always been done. However, it is increasingly a revisionist liberal brand of chicken plucking because it has been adapted to modern culture and society.

Chapter 2: The Method of Modern Chicken Plucking. Whereas classical or traditional chicken plucking was based on a transcendent model, modern chicken plucking contrasts with this in that it holds human beings to be the measure of all things.

Chapter 3: The Status of the Bible in Modern Chicken Plucking. This chapter will show that modern liberal chicken plucking is based on the record of supposed human experience of the divine and thus contains both the fallibility of humanity as well as the fate of being locked into historical and cultural situations.

Chapters 4, 5, 6 . . . : You get the idea.

Conclusion: Don't forget to add the conclusion.

The outline section is also the place where you can mention other details of the book, such as whether it will require maps, charts, graphs, photographs, tables, illustrations, or other specific images. This is also the place to tell the editor how many manuscript pages will be involved when the manuscript is complete. Also project when you plan to finish the writing and when you anticipate submitting the material.

Identify the Market

At this point in your proposal, turn your attention to the reading audience for your book project. Don't ever tell an editor that "everyone will want to read my book." That is nonsense. No one has a universal audience, not even the best and most popular writers of all time. Books are written to *specific* people, and you must have a specific reader in mind whom you want to reach.

Now, in thinking through the book's title, premise, and proposed outline, you have already gone a long way toward determining your book's ultimate reader, and no doubt you have a pretty good idea whom your book is for. But you should consider two more things in coming to terms with your reading audience: the *external* characteristics and the *internal* characteristics of your intended reader.

In considering the *external* characteristics of your audience, you are talking about *what* sort of person would buy your book, and this would include things like gender, age, economic status, religious affiliation, education level, and so on. Is your book for men, women, or both? Is it for singles, married people, or grandparents? Is it for the general reader, the student, or for the scholar? Is it for Christians or non-Christians? And so on. Considering the external characteristics of the reading audience for our book, *Chicken Plucking Today,* we might say something along these lines:

"This book is for adult evangelical Christians, including upper-division college students, first seminarians, busy clergy, and alert lay readers who are interested in what is happening in the field of chicken plucking."

In considering the *internal* characteristics of your audience, you are not talking about what sort of person would be interested in your book but rather *why* such a person would be interested. This would include such things as what a reader's needs and interests are and what he or she expects to get out of the book. Here is an example of what we could say about the internal characteristics of *Chicken Plucking Today* readers:

"Readers of *Chicken Plucking Today* will be those of stout mind and stout heart who fear for the health of evangelicalism in our country because they are aware of the inroads liberal chicken plucking is making into the church."

When you combine the external and internal statements, this will give your editor a fairly clear idea of the reading audience you have in mind. Beyond this, your statement on the reading audience—or market—for your book will give the editor a strong feeling whether his is the right publisher to reach the audience you have in mind.

The Competition

Now that you have considered the title, content, premise, outline, and reading audience for your book proposal, you need to give the editor an indication of what other books are available on the same topic, or a similar topic, on which you are writing. In other words, you need to know the competing titles that are already available in the marketplace. If you don't know what has already been published on the subject area in which you are writing, you are wasting your time and, worse yet, your editor's time. You may be writing a book that has already been written or a book that no one has ever written (perhaps because no one wants to read it).

Keep in mind that the editor wants to know if you have done your homework. She wants to know if there is a proven market for a book of the type you are proposing. If other books are available, you need to tell how your book differs from the others and why it is needed. For our book we might suggest this:

"Chicken plucking has been explored recently in *Doing Chicken Plucking in Today's World,* written by Carol Ediger and Lori Wagner and published seven years ago by Broadman & Holman Publishers; however, that book is far too advanced for the average Christian and could not be used at the entry level by students who bring no technical level of expertise in the field of chicken plucking. Beyond my book, *Chicken Plucking Today,* nothing is available."

Author Information

Now you have identified the competition and told the editor what ballpark you are playing in. And by now you have told him quite enough about your book project. Now it's time to tell him something abut you. Mention your background especially as it relates to the topic of the book you are currently writing. This will tell him you are qualified to write a book like *Chicken Plucking Today.* If you have won an award for chicken plucking, say so here. If you have earned academic degrees in chicken plucking, list them. List all your credentials and also your experience in the field of chicken plucking. Tell the editor why you are just the right person to write this book. If other matters are important—things that may be relevant to the research or the writing of this book—mention these as well.

If you have written other books on this topic, be sure to mention them. Or if you have written articles for magazines or journals or taught pertinent courses, be sure to mention these. Even if you are a first-time writer who has never published before, say so. That's OK. Everyone has to start somewhere.

CHAPTER 7

Touring the Publishing Contract

You have written your sample chapters, contacted a publisher with a thorough and well-done book proposal, and now you are camping out by your mailbox. One day the postman brings a strange looking document entitled "Letter of Agreement." Only after you read the thing four times do you realize it's a contract from the editor offering to publish your book. But now what?

The first thing *not* to do is run out and buy a Cadillac. Yes, you will probably make some money from your book but not enough to buy a new car—at least not right away. Support your writing habit until it supports you. Franz Kafka supported himself and his writing as an insurance salesman. Wallace Stevens did this as a lawyer. T. S. Eliot was a book editor, and Zane Grey, a dentist. Walt Whitman worked as a secretary for the Department of the Interior. Kurt Vonnegut did PR work for General Electric. John Steinbeck was a journalist. Dorothy Parker, Dorothy Sayers, and Aldous Huxley worked as copywriters, and O. Henry was a bank cashier before fleeing to South America after being charged with embezzlement! The message is, don't quit your day job.

Religious book sales in the United States will reach well beyond two billion dollars this year. You want your share of that total, but in all probability your share will be fairly small. Your rewards for writing will be something nobler than just money. As Harry Emerson Fosdick once said, "Across the years one of the most gratifying rewards of my ministry has been the stream of letters, often from out-of-the-way places all over the world, bearing messages of appreciation for help received from those earlier books of mine."[1] This is an all-important perspective to keep on your writing ministry. After all, anyone can make money, but not everyone can make a positive, lasting contribution to another's life.

Back to contracts. What you must do, instead of planning to spend your future earnings at this point, is to try to understand the nature of the publishing contract. It is simply the written record of an agreement—a memorial or reminder of an original agreement—agreed to and signed by the author and the publishing company. Each agreement has special needs, and therefore the contract should offer a clear and unambiguous understanding of all the terms of the agreement. Contracts deal with future uncertainty by providing advance solutions for predictable situations. They say, "Here's what we'll do together if we publish your book, if your book needs editing, or an index, if it needs revising, or if it sells more than fifty thousand copies, or someone sues us, or any number of other things occur."[2] There is no assurance that even when a publisher commits time and money to a publishing project there will ever be a return of investment. The agreement to write and publish a book is always a gamble for both the author and especially the publisher. Therefore, one way to look at the publishing contract is as an imperfect attempt at a fair division of the cost of losing and the rewards of winning.

If a publisher offers to publish your book, the contract offered you will no doubt agree to have the publisher pay all printing and production costs and to pay you specified royalties, among certain other standard matters. But remember, not every contract is the same. In this chapter we want to alert you to those areas on which you should concentrate. If you are offered a contract, the first thing to do is to read it carefully. Talk to a lawyer knowledgeable in literary law about it if you have any reservation. Some literary agents can also help.[3]

We are neither lawyers, nor are we experts on contracts, but we have seen our share of publishing agreements. Book publishing follows predictable patterns, and most of the publishing contracts you come across will be fairly standard. This is not to say that even standard contracts can't be modified. They can. Most publishers are willing to negotiate and to make certain changes in the contract. As the author, you should be aware of the more typical contract provisions as well as some of the variations that can be used. What we want to do here is give you a guided tour through a standard publishing agreement. There is probably no such thing as an ideal contract. Though most publishing contracts are much alike, with nearly fifty clauses that read about the same, the language and the terms will vary. The main thing is to understand the provisions of the agreement sent to you. There are certain basic elements in every contract—the important clauses—and that is where we will concentrate.

One last word before we begin looking at the sample contract. There is a notion that the publishing contract is always slanted in favor of the publisher. This is not true, or at least this should not be true. The purpose of the contract is not to put something over on anyone. This is not an adversarial process. Authors and publishers must protect themselves, but they should also be equitable.

Now, *please refer to the sample contract at the end of this chapter.*

The Standard Publishing Contract

Number 1 is a standard grant clause. The grant of rights clause allows the author to transfer some or all of the ownership of a work to a publisher, giving the publisher permission to publish the manuscript. This is the section of the contract where the author grants to the publisher the exclusive rights to publish and sell the book. This grant of rights may be limited as to geography, time, and language, or whatever else is called for in the contract. This clause tells you all the things your publisher can do with the work once it is bought. It will define whether the grant of rights to the publisher is complete and exclusive or is limited in one way or another. Many religious publishers will ask for a broad grant of rights so they are able to exercise all rights under the copyright for the "sole and exclusive right to print, publish, and sell" their edition of your book.

From the publisher's point of view, the basic starting point for the grant of rights is *all rights.* (The reason for this is easy to understand: the publisher finds it difficult to administer minor exceptions.) This is often unrealistic, however, and authors are seldom willing to grant such sweeping rights. That is why most contracts define carefully what rights are being assigned to the publisher and what rights are being reserved by the author. The "primary right" that an author grants to a publisher is the right to print the work in book form, and even the primary right can be limited according to the terms of the contract.

Publishers and authors both should be reasonable and not try to get more than they need in this clause. If a publisher has an active subsidiary rights department and is able effectively to get more income through rights sales, why not let the publisher have them? It is not unusual for a publisher to want to publish related or derivative products from a successful book or to want to publish the book in various versions (audio, electronic, etc.). And if an author or an agent insists on limiting a publisher's rights, it simply means the book is not as valuable. On the other hand, if the publishing house is not active in the sale of such rights, why do they need to ask for all rights?

A real matter of concern for writers of today is the question of electronic media. Be sure to have this spelled out in your contract in the grant of rights clause. Remember, if you have no protection, you have no rights.

Clause 2 allows the publisher to copyright the book in the author's name. Since all a publisher needs is the legal right to publish, and not necessarily ownership of the copyright itself, you will usually not find contract language that gives the publisher the right to take out the copyright in its own name. If you do find this language, keep in mind that most publishers do not mind if authors insist on having their books copyrighted in their names and not that of the publishing house, so this is sometimes an area of negotiation between an author and a publisher. If the copyright is to be kept in the author's name (where the author's name appears on the copyright page), the license to publish the book is then transferred to the publisher. If the publisher copyrights the book in its own name, then certain provisions are usually made in the contract for the copyright to revert to the author after certain things occur, such as the book going out of print.

Publishers normally take responsibility for handling the formalities of copyright. Keep in mind that the whole reason for the publishing contract is to transfer rights from author to publisher, allowing the latter to publish the material owned by the former. But even if the author grants all rights to the publisher, most publishing houses will as a legal matter copyright the work in the author's name.

Clause 4 is a warranties and indemnities clause, which is actually a protection used by publishers to indemnify themselves against possible lawsuits. The author certifies that the work is original and not plagiarized. The author further promises the publisher that he or she has every legal right to enter into a publishing agreement, and in so doing they are not interfering with anyone else's rights. Should these promises be breached, the author agrees to pay the publisher for any loss (cf. clause 26).

In the fifth clause the author agrees not to try to publish another book that would compete with the sale or impair sales of the work referred to in the contract. If the contracted work is anthologized sermons, for example, the author could not offer a condensed version of the anthology to another publisher.

The author agrees to secure any necessary grants of permission to quote copyrighted works in clause 6. The general rule is that permission must be granted for all material still under copyright unless it falls under the "fair use" doctrine of the Copyright Act, which permits a reasonable use of copyrighted material without the consent of the copyright proprietor. This is a nebulous concept, with no hard and fast rules, and authors need to remember to credit all copyrighted sources even when permissions are unnecessary. Since it is the author who knows what he or she has borrowed, it is sensible that the permissions responsibility should rest with the author and not the publisher.

Clause 7 stipulates that the author will read the galley proofs of the manuscript and return them promptly to the publisher. Most often a timetable for returning the proofs is listed here, whether two weeks or thirty days or whatever. This clause also stipulates that the author will not undertake a rewrite or otherwise try to make major changes or alterations in the manuscript at that time. The reason for this is that once the material is set in type in galley proof form, it is expensive to make such corrections. Galleys, by the way, are the tentative layout of the material in page form, the proofs being drawn from uncorrected copy set in a single column on which an author proofreads and marks any errors in the margins. The typesetter then goes back and makes any necessary corrections prior to page makeup.

The eighth clause spells out the deadline for delivery of the final copy of the manuscript to the publisher. (The original meaning of the word *deadline* meant the boundary around a prison beyond which no prisoner could go safely. If one stepped over the line, he was dead!) Many publishers are not that rigorous about the manuscript delivery date. With a publishing schedule, as with a writer's schedule, there will always be some slippage.

Remember, Murphy's Law always seems to prevail. Still, if an author has a legitimate reason for being late, usually all that is required is calling your editor and keeping the publishing house properly informed. But don't count on this in all cases. The delivery date is important because the publisher can terminate the contract if an author fails to get the manuscript to the editor in time. And if any advance money has been paid, the publisher can demand that it be returned. Authors should realize that publishers themselves operate under strict deadlines, and the late delivery of manuscripts can cause problems with editorial work schedules, the printing of catalogs and promotional pieces for the books, the work of field sales representatives, and with sales more generally. This is why, after a fair and reasonable time of delay (which general trade practice defines as no more than one or two months), most publishers do not fail to contact the author regarding late manuscripts. If extensions are granted, then both sides should make definite new delivery date guidelines. Most writers will admit that the deadline is a wonderful discipline, and they are thankful to get one.

The ninth clause is directly related to the preceding one. It gives the publisher the right to terminate the contract should the author fail to deliver the manuscript within a specified period of time from the stated delivery date. Publishers must set the schedule for publication. They also realize that if they wait too long after the material under contract slides by the delivery date, they may have to waive the right to cancel the contract. That is why manuscript delivery and the time limit for publication are so important. All of this means that when the manuscript is due, most publishing houses will call it in.

The author agrees in clause 10 to provide an index if the publisher wants one. This is often a matter of negotiation too. The publisher can provide an index as easily as the author.

Clause 11 gives the publisher the right to edit the work. This is extremely important since it indicates who has the last say about what appears in the book. It is entirely standard for a publisher's contract to insist on the house's right to change the written material to fit its own editorial style. If you as the author wish final editorial control of everything in your book, you must be sure to amend the contract to say so. However, such a position is highly impractical for all but a few well-established writers. It is best that you require of your editor that he or she consult with you regarding all changes, including the change of title. This also can be added to the contract.

The twelfth clause is the publisher's agreement to publish, which tells the author when to expect publication of the book once the manuscript is delivered in satisfactory condition. Usually an author can expect the finished book within twelve to eighteen months after the manuscript has been approved, depending of course on the publisher's schedule and on what sort of editing, typesetting method, graphics, and printing technology are to be used by the publisher on the particular book project.

Clause 13 is *the* crucial paragraph for many authors. A royalty is a payment made to the author in exchange for granting the publisher the right to publish and sell your book. Sometimes a publisher will offer an author a one-time payment for a work, and in this case there is no continuing royalty payment. But most book publishing operates with a continuing royalty arrangement calculated as a percentage of the publisher's income from the sale of the book. The royalty is calculated in different ways, and it is of utmost importance to understand what this portion of your contract says.

Most publishing contracts stipulate a royalty rate of a certain percentage on the *net* sales of the book (usually 14 to 16 or 18 percent of net sales on a trade book). This means that the royalty will be figured on what the publisher receives from bookstores, libraries, distributors, book clubs, and other places where the book is sold. Let's say a book retails for $15.99. The royalty rate is not based on that figure, however. It is based on the price given to outlets. To certain accounts, a discount of 40 percent is common. This means that the author would receive a royalty based on $9.59 instead of the $15.99 list price. In other words, the author is given 14 percent or 16 percent (or whatever the contract calls for) of whatever the publisher receives for the sale of the book. This is a fair and clean arrangement, and it is easy to police. In this way, the available royalty money is figured on the basis of what the publisher actually *receives* from the sale of the book to all the various sales channels the publisher uses.

A few publishers offer a basic royalty rate based on the suggested *retail* price of a book, with rates for paperbacks commonly a bit lower than for hardcovers. While it may seem that this arrangement favors the author more than the one based on the net price (the royalty payment being based on the retail price of the book, which is higher than the net price), the fact is that publishers almost never sell books at the retail or list price. Consequently, this system of royalty payment is highly irregular anymore. It is better to figure the available royalty money on the basis of what the publisher actually *receives* from the sale of the book.

Letters *a* through *m* of clause 13 in the sample contract spell out in detail what royalties will be paid under certain conditions. These stipulations are often found in standard contracts. Authors and agents should pay far more attention to these adjustment provisions than they normally do. Remember, the matter of royalty percentage payment is as open to negotiation as anything else in a publishing contract. Remember also that some advance money is often paid to the author either at the time of contract signing or when the final manuscript is submitted (or a combination of both), but the advance money is always debited against future royalty earnings.

Clause 14 stipulates what subsidiary rights belong to the publisher. This section of the contract could be called "Subsidiary Rights" or "Rights Conveyed" or "Grant of Rights." Your contract will detail exactly what subsidiary rights belong to the publisher and which belong to you as the author. As we mentioned in the Standard Grant Clause (1), publishers like to begin by seeking *all rights*. If you find this unrealistic because you might want to keep, for example, television or movie or audio/video rights, this should be spelled out.

These rights are called "subsidiary rights" or "sub rights" because they are usually subsidiary in importance—less important than the primary right you initially give the publisher to publish and sell your book. However, as you can see from the sample contract under section 14, the area of sub rights includes a wide variety of media, some of which could actually prove more valuable than the right to publish the book in traditional form. In most cases you will not be too concerned about your book being made into a movie!

Clauses 15 through 18 explain in greater detail other matters related to royalties and payments. Most contracts in book publishing provide for royalty accounts to be computed annually or semiannually, with payments figured "less returns." Returns are those books a bookseller returns to the publisher for credit because they failed to sell. Returns certainly affect royalty payments to authors because a publisher does not want to pay royalty based on a large number of books originally shipped if a significant portion of unsold books will be returned a few months later. So most publishers have a "reserve against returns" clause, with the sort of wording you will see in section 15. This allows the publisher to withhold part of the author's royalties for a specified period of time (since publishers only allow bookstores to return books for a specified period of time). For books sold in the general bookstore trade, a "reasonable reserve" in these matters is usually based on a return rate of 30 to 40 percent of the books shipped. Be sure you try to get this spelled out.

Clause 19 in the sample contract does not include any type of insurance on the part of the author. But things are changing. All major publishing houses now buy defamation and liability insurance for themselves, and a growing number are now providing similar protection for their authors. This arrangement is a fairly recent addition to some publishing agreements.

Section 22 is the "termination" or "remainder and out-of-print clause." This language gives the publisher the prerogative of declaring the book out of print when the demand for the work "shall not . . . be sufficient to render its publication profitable." When a publisher declares a book out of print, due to the demand for the book dropping to the point the publisher cannot justify reprinting it and keeping it in the marketplace, the rights in most cases go back to the author. There should always be a written document to verify that the transfer of rights has been given. Since the publisher will declare a title out of print usually when a book has failed to sell a specified number of copies within a stated period of time, authors are wise if they can get this number and period of time stated in their contract. The author should ask the publisher to be specific in this area.

In virtually all publishing agreements, the author has the right to buy unsold copies of the book, usually at a deep discount, before it is remaindered, along with the plates and negatives in some cases, if the author wishes. With this option the author can then sell the book to another publisher or even self-publish it. Therefore, the author may be able to purchase remaindered copies as well as recover the copyright or publication license at the same time.

"Remaindering" is a way the publisher can sell remaining copies of a book from the publisher's inventory at a fraction of the actual cost or worth. Put another way, publishers reserve the right to discontinue publication and to dispose of unsold copies at a low ("remainder") price. This is almost always a last-ditch effort for the publisher since books are remaindered only after the publisher has determined they can be sold no other way. The publisher is usually required to notify the author if they determine that the book must be remaindered. Many publishers will allow an author to require that the book not be remaindered for a designated period of time after its publication. If you can negotiate that sort of language in your contract, you should do it. But all published books are subject to remaindering if in the long run they do not continue to sell.

In clause 23, the contract states how many complimentary copies of the finished book the author gets for personal use. Most contracts contain such a clause. The important thing here, though, is not the number of free copies the author is allowed (it's usually anywhere from fifteen to fifty), but the price at which the author can purchase additional copies of the book from the publisher. This buy-back option is important for many writers who lecture or otherwise offer their own books for sale to the public through their appearances. Usually the publisher will insist on paying a more limited royalty on buy-backs—or no royalty at all—if the author wishes a more generous discount on the books bought back for resale. Again, the discount is a matter for negotiation.

While the language in our sample contract does not suggest this, in many contracts this clause would prohibit authors from reselling their author's copies. If an author makes personal appearances, speaks on the lecture circuit, or has other opportunities to make direct sales of their books, they should ask to have such prohibition against resale language dropped. Most publishers are open to permitting resale so long as the initial sale of copies to the author is royalty-free and there is a guarantee no copies will be sold into the retail market where they would compete with the publisher's sales. In this way the author is not earning a royalty when buying copies of their own book, but they are allowed to resell the book at their personal appearances and keep the difference between the wholesale and retail prices.

Clause 24, the option or the right of first refusal, is another key clause. It is understandable that a publisher who takes a chance on one book project by an author wants to tie that author to the house for a possible future project. The publisher naturally wants to participate in an author's success by gaining the right to publish the author's subsequent book and reaping the benefit of a developing readership waiting for the next publication. The publisher can do this through two contract clauses, "the option clause" and "the right of first refusal clause."

The option clause is certainly the more forceful clause from the publisher's point of view. It requires the author to sell his or her next book to the same publisher on the same terms of the present contract unless there is mutual agreement to other terms. Under the option clause, the author may not submit any future book to another publisher until after the original publisher has made a publishing decision. Most authors will wish to vigorously negotiate this type of clause, thinking of it in the nature of indentured servitude.

Perhaps a more reasonable clause, at least from the author's point of view, is the right of first refusal clause. In this type of agreement, the author has to allow the original publisher the "first chance" at the author's next book project. Sometimes the publisher asks that it also be given a second chance—to match a better deal given the author by another publishing firm. A third variant of the option clause is the "capping rights" or the "right of last refusal." This gives the publisher one last chance to make a deal with the author by taking into account all other publishers' offers and trying to top them. The terms of these rights to first, second, and last refusals, including the response time a publisher has to make a decision, are open to negotiation. Negotiation is usually much more difficult under an option clause.

As an author you would be better off either to negotiate the removal of these clauses altogether, if you can, or to sign a right of first refusal clause with a short publisher's response time. We have heard of some writers who purposely keep a "terrible" manuscript around for the sole purpose of living up to the letter of the law in such a right of first refusal clause. They say they know it is so bad that no publisher could possibly want it. After offering the terrible manuscript to the original publisher upon the publication of a first book, they can then turn to other houses to negotiate other projects as they wish. (Of course this rarely happens in Christian publishing!)

The assignment clause in section 25 is contained in all publishing contracts. It protects both the publisher and the author should either wish to transfer the contract rights to another party, which transfer of rights has to be in writing. Assignments can occur when an author designates that the income from a book is to be paid to a creditor, for example, or when a publishing company sells its book list to another publisher, or when the company itself goes out of business. Usually a publisher keeps the right to make assignments unilaterally, but when the author wishes to assign rights or royalties to a third party, the publisher typically reserves the right to agree with the assignment for it to be valid.

Clause 26, on suits for infringement of copyright, is related to section 4, the author's guarantee. Both sections have to do with copyright infringements and possible legal action taken against the author or the publisher. Generally, a copyright infringement suit is brought in the name of the person owning or controlling the rights that have been infringed, and it is brought against the person thought to be infringing the rights. What is important in this section is to see if the author or the publisher, or both equally, takes the financial burden if someone makes a claim of infringement of copyright on the work. As the author, you should ask for an infringement provision in your contract that limits your financial liability to claims considered by a court. Otherwise, you could be held liable by the publisher for legal costs involved in claims that are bogus. Often, a publisher will withhold royalty payments pending the outcome of a lawsuit. You need to know how much of the entire royalty is to be withheld and for how long. Also, find out if you are liable for any agreed-upon amount in the event that a judgment is made for the claimant.

A promotion clause, such as in section 28 in the sample contract, is typical of publishing contracts. The right to use an author's name is implied in the other terms and conditions of the contract, though what is included in this section depends on the size and kind of publisher you deal with. Many larger Christian houses commit large sums of money for publicity and advertising campaigns, including author tours, media appearances, and bookstore signing parties. But all houses, however large or small, will want to promote an author's work by using the author's name, photo, and biographical summary. The typical publishing contract will give the publisher this right.

When signing a book contract, the author bestows on the publisher the "right of publicity," giving the publisher the right to decide how and when to use the author's name in the promotion of the book. If you do not wish to give your publisher promotional rights without restriction, this will need to be so stated in this section of your contract.

Some publishers wish to require the author to assist in certain promotions. In that case, the contract should clearly state whatever obligation in this regard is required and which party bears the expenses. If there are some things you definitely would or would not do in the publicity and promotion of your book, these should be spelled out in this section of the contract.

The "law applicable" or "governing law" clause of section 29 can be a headache for an author who lives in one state while his or her publisher's office is in another state. This clause simply specifies what body of law will apply in a legal dispute between the publisher and the author. It means that the author must agree to tackle whatever legal hassles ensue from the book in the publisher's state. The author cannot be sued in his or her own state since through this clause they agree that jurisdiction over disputes will always be in the publisher's home state. Many lawyers who practice literary law prefer the law of the state of New York since much of the case law concerning the publishing industry has been decided in New York courts.

Remember that this "choice of law" clause does not determine *where* a lawsuit must be filed. The venue and jurisdiction of a suit usually cannot be chosen by the parties to a publishing contract—a number of other factors determine these things.

This sample contract has a provision for other stipulations, which is what the amendments clause 32 is about. It is added to the existing agreements already given and allows either party by mutual consent to add other matters that they wish to specify. Normally, all changes in the contract terms are to be in writing (oral agreements are *not* effective) and signed by the party against whom the new terms are to be enforced. Authors should *always* have a confirming letter signed by the publisher.

For Further Assistance

Most large city bar associations have committees of specialists in literary law and intellectual property law. These committees often are willing to offer inexpensive legal work, sometimes even *pro bono* work, for authors unable to pay much for legal services. For referrals you can call the bar association and ask for the name of the chairperson of the appropriate committee.[4]

Any contract you sign with a publisher is an important, formidable document that could have a serious impact on your future. Be careful. Read it carefully and, if necessary, check it out with someone who knows publishing or literary law. While it pays to be cautious, remember that reputable publishers have no desire to rip you off or to create bad feelings between themselves and you. Publishers live off the output of writers, so the relationship between the publisher and the author must be a symbiotic one. Most publishers want to cultivate a good working relationship with an author because if that writer's books sell, the publisher will want more of them.

We hope you and your publisher come to a meeting of the minds with a contract accommodating the needs and expectations of both parties and that your first contract is signed, sealed, and delivered very soon.

Sample PUBLISHING AGREEMENT

Frumious Bandersnatch, Inc., Publishers

AGREEMENT made this ___ day, of ___ 20 ___ between Frumious Bandersnatch, Inc., Publishers of Nashville, Tennessee, hereinafter called the PUBLISHER, and _____

whose address is _____

and _____

whose address is _____

(herein referred to, whether one or more, as AUTHOR), being the proprietor(s) of a work provisionally entitled _____

_____

(hereinafter referred to as the WORK).

Grant

1. In consideration of the stipulations and covenants of the respective parties hereto, the AUTHOR hereby grants to the PUBLISHER its successors and assigns, the sole and exclusive right to publish and sell, or license the publication and sale of the above work in book form throughout the world during the full term of copyright and all renewals and extensions thereof, including the subsidiary rights hereinafter specified.

Copyright

2. The PUBLISHER, at its discretion, will register copyright to the WORK within three (3) months of publication in the name of the AUTHOR in accordance with the requirements of the copyright law of the United States. The PUBLISHER will take reasonable care to affix the proper copyright notice to each copy of the WORK.

Amendment of Law

3. All references to copyright made in this agreement are subject to such amendment and change as may be enacted by the Congress of the United States of America or by any other legal authority with regard to the present Copyright Act or by the adoption of any new Copyright Act.

Author's Guarantee

4. The AUTHOR certifies to the PUBLISHER that he is the sole author and proprietor of said work; that the work is original and does not infringe upon the statutory copyright or upon any common law right, proprietary right or any other right whatsoever; that it contains nothing of an objectionable or libelous character; that the work is not in violation of any right of privacy; and that he and/or his legal representative shall and will hold harmless and keep indemnified the PUBLISHER from all suits and all manner of claims, proceedings and expenses, including attorney's fees, which may be taken or incurred on the ground that said work is such a violation, or contains something objectionable or libelous or otherwise unlawful. The AUTHOR undertakes for himself, his heirs and assigns, to execute at any time, on request of the PUBLISHER, any document or documents to confirm or continue any of the rights defined herein. AUTHOR guarantees that WORK has not heretofore been published; that he is the sole and exclusive owner of the rights herein granted to the PUBLISHER; and that he has not heretofore assigned, pledged, or otherwise encumbered the same.

Competing Edition

5. The AUTHOR shall not, without the consent of the PUBLISHER, publish any abridged or other edition of said work or any book of similar or competing character tending to interfere with the sale of the work covered by this agreement.

Permissions

6. If copyright material from other sources is included in the work, the AUTHOR shall, at his own expense, obtain from the copyright

owners or their representatives written permission for use of such material, and shall deliver such permissions at the time of delivery of the final manuscript.

Author Proofs

7. The AUTHOR agrees to read and correct the galley and page proofs and return them to the PUBLISHER in such time and manner as will not delay the printer, and to pay, as a charge against royalties, or, at the option of the PUBLISHER, in cash, the expense of any alterations or additions authorized by the AUTHOR (other than those due to printer's errors) in the proof in excess of ten percent (10%) of the cost of composition of the said work as originally supplied by the AUTHOR, but in no case shall the PUBLISHER share of this cost exceed fifty dollars ($50.00), except by mutual and express consent.

Delivery of final manuscript

8. The AUTHOR agrees to deliver into the hands of the PUBLISHER on or before the day of _____ 20__ a final revised copy of the manuscript, legibly typewritten and satisfactory to the PUBLISHER in content and form and ready to print from, including all charts, drawings, designs, photographs, and illustrations which are referred to in the text and intended to be a part thereof suitable for use by the PUBLISHER in preparing copies for reproduction. In event the AUTHOR chooses not to deliver such charts, drawings, designs, photographs, and illustrations, the PUBLISHER may supply them, charging the cost thereof against and deducting it from any or all monies accruing to the AUTHOR under this and/or other agreements between the AUTHOR and the PUBLISHER.

The PUBLISHER may with the consent of the AUTHOR supply charts, drawings, designs, photographs, and illustrations, which in their opinion are necessary to the content, promotion, and distribution of said work, charging the cost thereof against and deducting it from any or all monies accruing to the AUTHOR under this and/or other agreements between the AUTHOR and the PUBLISHER, except the cost of engraving and printing.

The length of the manuscript shall be approximately _____ words, and shall contain the following kind and approximate number of illustrations: _____

Time Limit for Publication

9. If, within the time specified in paragraph 8, such manuscript and support material is not delivered, the PUBLISHER shall not be bound by the time limit of publication hereinafter provided for, and in the event the manuscript is not delivered within three (3) months after delivery date specified in Paragraph 8, the PUBLISHER shall have the right of election to continue this agreement in effect or to terminate it and to receive back from the AUTHOR any monies paid or expended hereunder.

Index

10. If the PUBLISHER requests, the AUTHOR agrees to supply within fifteen (15) days after final page proof of the text has been submitted by the PUBLISHER, an index in proper content and form and ready to set type therefrom. If the AUTHOR fails to do so, the PUBLISHER may have one prepared and charge the cost thereof to the AUTHOR.

Editing

11. The text and illustrations of said WORK shall be subject to editing and revision by the PUBLISHER prior to first publication, or to any subsequent printing, provided, however, that such editing or revision shall not materially change the meaning, or materially alter the text of said WORK without the AUTHOR'S consent. Editing to correct infelicities of expression, misstatements of fact, misquotations, errors in grammar, sentence structure, and spelling, and editing to make the WORK conform to the PUBLISHER'S style of punctuation, capitalization, and like details, shall not be considered as material changes.

Publisher's Agreement to Publish

12. The PUBLISHER agrees to publish said WORK at its own expense, not later than eighteen (18) months from the date of receipt of satisfactory manuscript, unless specified otherwise in this agreement in such style, and at such price as the PUBLISHER shall determine as best suited to its success (including special prepublication price, if any). It is understood that advertising, number and destination of free copies, and all details of manufacture and publication shall be in the exclusive control of the PUBLISHER, and the stock of plates and books shall be the property of the PUBLISHER.

Royalty

13. The PUBLISHER shall pay to the AUTHOR royalty as follows:

(a) Ten percent (10%) of the net sales on all copies of the regular trade edition (except as noted hereinafter) sold by the PUBLISHER within the United States of America (by *net sales* is meant gross receipts less discounts to the trade);

(b) Five percent (5%) of net sales of the paperback edition sold by the PUBLISHER within the United States of America (by *net sales* is meant gross receipts less discounts to the trade).

(c) When in its judgment it is necessary or advisable, the PUBLISHER is authorized to sell copies of the WORK at a discount of fifty percent (50%) or more. When copies are sold at discounts of fifty percent (50%) or more, a royalty of five percent (5%) of net sales shall be paid to the AUTHOR.

(d) When copies are sold by the PUBLISHER through mail order, coupon advertising, or radio or television advertising, the royalty shall be five percent (5%) of the amount received therefrom, excluding postage and other handling charges.

(e) For the purpose of keeping the WORK in print and in circulation as long as possible, the AUTHOR agrees that, after two (2) years from the date of first publication of the regular trade edition, if in any twelve (12)-month period the sales do not exceed two hundred and fifty (250) copies, the royalty shall be one-half of the prevailing rate.

(f) The PUBLISHER shall have the right to arrange for foreign editions of said work, paying the AUTHOR fifty percent (50%) of the net payments received by the PUBLISHER.

(g) The PUBLISHER shall have the right to make arrangements for sales of American edition copies of the WORK outside the continental limits of the United States and its dependencies, paying the AUTHOR on such sales a royalty of ten percent (10%) of the amount actually received by the PUBLISHER.

(h) On copies of any cheap edition published by another firm, for which the PUBLISHER shall have the exclusive right to arrange, the AUTHOR shall receive fifty percent (50%) of the amount received by the PUBLISHER. Royalties on any cheap edition issued by the PUBLISHER shall be fixed by agreement between the AUTHOR and the PUBLISHER.

(i) On copies of a textbook edition at a reduced suggested retail selling price issued for sale to educational institutions, a royalty of five percent (5%) of the textbook suggested retail selling price shall be paid to the AUTHOR.

(j) On bound copies sold from PUBLISHER'S stock to or through recognized book clubs, a royalty of five percent (5%) of the suggested retail selling price shall be paid to the AUTHOR, provided, however, in the case of copies sold through the PUBLISHER'S recognized book clubs for use as one of two or more books offered as a main selection, the royalty shall be one-half of the aforementioned royalty; and provided, further, in the case of copies used as bonus or introductory offers in the PUBLISHER'S recognized book clubs, no royalty shall be paid.

(k) The PUBLISHER shall have the exclusive right to make arrangements with recognized book clubs granting them permission to print special editions of the WORK. Compensation for such rights shall be divided equally between AUTHOR and PUBLISHER.

(l) On the sale of sheet stock from the American edition sold to a foreign publisher, the AUTHOR shall be compensated at the rate of ten percent (10%) of the net amount received by the PUBLISHER.

(m) No royalties shall be paid upon copies given to the AUTHOR, salesmen's samples, damaged copies, returned copies, copies given away to publicize the WORK or to promote sales, or copies sold at or below manufacturing costs as determined by the PUBLISHER.

Subsidiary Rights

14. The following shall be considered as subsidiary rights, for the sale of which the PUBLISHER shall be solely responsible; serial rights before and after book publication; dramatic, public reading and other nondramatic performing rights; motion picture rights; translations, digests, abridgements, selections and anthologies; also mechanical, visual such as microfilm and micropoint (other than motion picture), sound reproducing and recording rights (including but not limited to television and broadcasting, phonographic, wire, tape, video, and electronic video recordings other than motion pictures); lyric rights and adaptions of said WORK for commercial use. The division of receipts from the sales of subsidiary rights shall be as follows:

(a) Except as provided in (c) and (d) of section 13, fifty percent (50%) to the AUTHOR and fifty percent (50%) to the PUBLISHER.

(b) Dramatic and/or motion picture, television and broadcasting rights, and adaptations for commercial use: seventy-five per-cent (75%) to the AUTHOR and twenty-five percent (25%) to the PUBLISHER of the amount received by the PUBLISHER.

(c)   The PUBLISHER is authorized to grant permission, at no charge and without paying royalty, for use of the work, or selections therefrom, by recognized organizations for the physically disabled.

Royalty Payments

15. Royalty accounts shall be computed annually to the first (1) day of April of each year, and statements thereof shall be rendered and the amount shown due thereby paid on or before the thirtieth (30) day of the following June. However, if in the opinion of the PUBLISHER, there is a risk of booksellers returning for credit a substantial quantity of unsold copies of the WORK, the PUBLISHER may withhold a reasonable reserve with which to compensate for such returns.

First Royalty Statement

16. If the WORK shall have been on sale for a period of time shorter than three months as of April I of a given year, the first statement shall be postponed until the next succeeding April I for computation.

Accounts Due Publisher

17. The AUTHOR agrees that any account, bills, advances, or amounts of any nature that may be due the PUBLISHER by the AUTHOR, whether under this agreement or not, shall be chargeable against and may be deducted from any or all monies accruing to the AUTHOR under this and/or other agreements between the AUTHOR and the PUBLISHER.

Taxes on Royalties

18. It is mutually agreed that any taxes, domestic or foreign, which are or may be levied on the AUTHOR'S royalties, when paid by the PUBLISHER are proper charges against the royalty earnings due under this agreement, and may be withheld by the PUBLISHER.

Insurance

19. No insurance whatever need be effected by the PUBLISHER for the AUTHOR.

Properly Spacing Author's Books

20. For the purpose of orderly and systematically promoting the AUTHOR'S reputation and acceptance as a writer, the PUBLISHER agrees not to publish this WORK until six months shall have elapsed since publication of the AUTHOR'S next preceding book, whether the next preceding book was published by the PUBLISHER or not, and the AUTHOR agrees that he will not permit his succeeding book to be published until six months shall have elapsed after publication of this WORK, whether the next succeeding book be published by the PUBLISHER or not.

Unavoidable Delay

21. It is mutually agreed that neither the AUTHOR nor the PUB-LISHER shall be held responsible for any delays which may be due to abnormal conditions existing in manufacturing, publishing, and distribution of books, including shortages in manufacturing facilities, personnel, and materials.

Termination

22. If at any time during the continuance of this agreement the demand for the WORK shall not, in the opinion of the PUBLISHER, be sufficient to render its publication profitable and it wishes to discontinue permanently the publication of said WORK, the AUTHOR shall have the right to buy from the PUBLISHER as an entirety all copies on hand at the cost of the manufacture and the stamps, electrotype plates and engravings of illustrations (if in existence) at actual cost to the PUBLISHER, including the composition. If the AUTHOR fails to exercise this option by paying for the same in cash within thirty (30) days after notice has been mailed to him by the PUBLISHER to his latest known address by registered mail, the PUBLISHER may destroy or dispose of the same as it sees fit without commission or percentage, and this agreement shall forthwith cease and terminate.

Author Copies

23. The PUBLISHER will furnish ten (10) copies of the published WORK to the AUTHOR at no charge. Should the AUTHOR desire additional copies for personal use, they shall be supplied at forty percent (40%) discount from the suggested retail selling price, carriage additional.

Right of First Refusal

24. The AUTHOR grants the PUBLISHER the right of first refusal on his next work. The AUTHOR shall not offer the same to someone else on more favorable terms without first offering the same to PUBLISHER on the same terms. Such option shall be exercised within ninety (90) days after the receipt by the PUBLISHER of the complete and final manuscript; provided, however, that in no case shall the PUBLISHER be obligated to accept or decline such manuscript earlier than ninety (90) days after the publication of the WORK covered by this agreement. Should the PUBLISHER decline the first manuscript so offered under the option, the AUTHOR is relieved of obligation for further submission.

Assignment

25. This agreement may be assigned but only in its entirety and shall be binding upon and inure to the benefit of the personal representatives and assigns of the AUTHOR and upon and to the successors and assigns of the PUBLISHER. No assignment shall be valid, as against the PUBLISHER, unless a copy or duplicate original of the same shall have been filed with the PUBLISHER.

Suits for Infringement of Copyright

26. If the copyright of the WORK is infringed, and if the parties proceed jointly, the expenses and recoveries, if any, shall be shared equally; and if they do not proceed jointly, either party shall have the right to prosecute such action, and such party shall bear all the expenses thereof, and any recoveries shall belong to such party; and if such party shall not hold the record title of the copyright, the other party shall permit the action to be brought in his or its name.

Sums Due and Owing

27. Any sums due and owing from the AUTHOR to the PUBLISHER, whether or not arising out of this agreement, may be deducted from any sum due, or that may become due from the PUBLISHER to the AUTHOR pursuant to this agreement.

Author's Name, Likeness, etc.

28. In connection with the publication, advertising, and marketing of the WORK, PUBLISHER shall, without restriction, have the right to use, and allow others to use, AUTHOR'S name, signature, and likeness, and biographic material concerning AUTHOR.

Law Applicable

29. This agreement shall be interpreted according to the law of the State of _____ regardless of the places of its physical execution.

Modification

30. This agreement constitutes the complete understanding of the parties. No modification or waiver of any provision shall be valid unless in writing and signed by both parties. The waiver of a breach of any of the terms hereof or any default hereunder shall not be deemed a waiver of any subsequent breach or default, whether of the same or similar nature, and shall not in any way affect the other terms hereof.

Limitation of Agreement

31. This agreement shall not be binding upon either the PUBLISHER or the AUTHOR unless it is signed by all and delivered to the PUBLISHER within a period of forty-five (45) days from the date of this agreement.

Amendments

32. This contract contains a memorandum of all the agreements, expressed or implied, between the parties hereto, but may be amended at any time by mutual consent of the parties hereto, but only in writing, signed by both parties and affixed to this contract and made a part thereof.

The changes, alterations, interlineations, and deletions made in Paragraphs _____ of this contract, and the additional typed clauses numbered _____ were made and added before the execution hereof.

Notice provision: Any notice to be given hereunder shall be sent by registered or certified mail, return receipt requested, addressed to the parties at their respective addresses above given. Either party may designate a different address by notice so given. IN WITNESS WHEREOF the parties have duly executed this agreement the day and year first above written.

_____   _____

Author's Signature   Publisher's Signature

Notes

1. Harry Emerson Fosdick, *The Living of These Days* (New York: Harper & Row, 1956), 135.

2. The publishing contract (or at least an implied contract) is also the only legal remedy for the misappropriation of ideas. For a good discussion of idea protection, with interesting examples, see *Intellectual Property Handbook, Fifth Edition* (Philadelphia: Morgan, Lewis & Bockius, LLP., 2000).

3. There are many helpful guides for the working writer on the publishing contract, including Ted Crawford's *The Writers Legal Guide,* Kirk Poking and Leonard S. Meranus's *Law and the Writer,* Brad Bunnin and Peter Beren's *Author Law & Strategies,* Richard Balkin's *A Writer's Guide to Contract Negotiations,* Linda F. Pinkerton's *The Writer's Law Primer,* and Jonathan Kirsch's, *Kirsch's Handbook of Publishing Law.*

4. Some helpful names and addresses are included in several of the resources mentioned above.

CHAPTER 8
The Publishing Process, or How to Commit Publishing

Where should we start in discussing the publishing process? We could talk about how books are created or how they are manufactured. We could talk about how books are marketed and sold or how they are delivered to bookstores around the country. We could talk about the anatomy of a publishing house, that is, who does what in editing, marketing, design, and sales. With a topic like the publishing process, we could even discuss how publishers do their business in financing books, planning publishing lists, and keeping their doors open for business. In thinking of the publishing process, one might consider the various trends that are hot today or how one could tailor a book idea to a specific reading market or how an editor evaluates a book proposal. With a topic like this, we could even talk about the future of Christian book publishing. This subject could go in many different directions.

But what we want to do in this chapter is reveal what happens to a manuscript when it is processed by a publisher. In other words, how is a manuscript turned into a finished book?

How Is a Manuscript Turned into a Finished Book?

You have spent a good part of your life giving birth to a manuscript. You have written and rewritten and rewritten again. You have tweaked it every which way but loose. Then, when the material was in the best shape you could put it in, you set out to find just the right publisher. You determined what category your book fit into, and you found solid reference material to help you do the market research to locate publishers that publish the kind of book you are writing. (If you didn't do this, you better read chapter 6 again on constructing the book proposal.) Lo and behold, you found a publisher who responded favorably to your carefully worded query letter and book proposal and asked to see your material. After you sent in samples, and after an extended period of review, the publisher reacted positively to what you sent. In fact, they said they wanted to publish it! After some negotiations, they offered you a contract, the terms of which you probably did not entirely like but nevertheless accepted. You and your editor agreed on a submission date for the final, finished manuscript. On or before the deadline, you submitted the manuscript. Now what?

Now the real fun begins. First, keep in mind that what happens to *your* manuscript and what happens to a manuscript authored by, say, a Rick Warren or a Beth Moore can differ as much as day differs from night! Why? Doesn't a publisher process each manuscript in exactly the same way? The answer is no. Publishers need to set their priorities like everyone else in business. This means they have to determine which books are more vital to their well-being, and it means they have to decide what amount of time, energy, and money needs to go into each book project. Naturally, the greater the sales potential a book has, the more time, energy, and money a publisher is willing to spend in producing, advertising, promoting, marketing, and selling the book. So when you consider making books and processing manuscripts, the first thing you have to know is that what happens depends a good deal on the available manpower and money that a publisher is willing to spend on the book. Editorial and book production work, then, is done on a priority basis.

Some of the questions an editor might ask when considering the editorial and production work schedule on your book might be these: Is it absolutely important for the book to appear during the next publishing season? Is your book a specialized one that will appeal to a limited reading audience? Is your manuscript overly long or complex? Will your manuscript require nine months before finished books can be shopped to the bookstores? Eighteen months? What amount of editing is required? Will the publisher assign an experienced senior editor to the project or a junior editor still learning the craft of editing? Does the publisher have a rosy picture of sales projects, or a bleak one? The answers to all these and other questions will determine what happens to a manuscript when it is processed by a publisher. The answers will determine which house staff are assigned to a project—and when.

Even though the actual number of editorial and production hours spent on your book may add up only to several weeks of work, the incubation period for the typical book is about nine months to a year.

Substantive Editing

What happens to your contracted manuscript when you send it in? What does your editor do before your manuscript is transmitted to the copyediting and production departments? First, there is substantive editing. This is when the editor reads the entire manuscript to double-check it and see if it's in acceptable shape. Many wonderful manuscripts turn out to have things wrong with them in substance or meaning. Maybe the fifth chapter makes no sense. Maybe the conclusion is weak. Maybe you forgot to add an important piece of information about your topic. At this point, light or heavy revisions could be suggested. In any event, the editor's first task is to read the finished manuscript and do what is called a substantive editing—which is the study of the text of a given manuscript to come to terms with the overall intent of the material and to determine if the writing has in any way fallen short.

It is the editor's function not to change the book or write the book herself; rather, the editor tries to read the manuscript in an objective way to act as a catalyst and a sounding board for the author. The sponsoring or acquiring editor (or editorial director, or editor in chief—there are many different titles) reads the material submitted for publication to see if it makes any sense and is in good shape. Often, the editor relies on the critical review of others, and this is especially true in the world of academic books. But one way or another the editor has to do his homework on the manuscript. It is important for you, the author, to know that the editor's substantive editing may enlarge or reduce or otherwise change your manuscript.

Reviews

On the topic of outside evaluations or reviews, many editors find they are not in the best position to finally approve a manuscript for publication. So, as a precaution, they have other people take a look. As we have said, this is the case with many books published in academic or scholarly areas, for most of these books contain information requiring a technical level of expertise the editor doesn't begin to possess. Getting a reader's report of three to five pages with comments about the manuscript's strengths and weaknesses is done with other types of books as well, for example with controversial books or with books on topics currently in the news.

The readers or reviewers will advise the editor on what revisions, if any, seem to be required. Editors rely a good deal on trusted outside reviewers. Usually, the identity of the outside reader is not disclosed to the author in order to guarantee anonymity. Therefore, reviewers can read as objectively as possible. If alert, qualified readers think something is amiss with your manuscript, the editor will usually believe them and then let you know what should be done. Remember that your contract will always state you are to deliver an acceptable manuscript, and what is "acceptable" is determined by the publisher, never the author.

Permissions/Rights

If your manuscript contains things quoted or otherwise used from other published sources (for example, maps, charts, illustrations, or lengthy quotes), the editor has to be careful that you have obtained the proper permissions in order to use this material. In most cases, you are required to get permission from other publishers to reprint copyrighted material in your book. In some publishing houses, this is handled by the person in charge of the rights and permissions department, and in other houses this is handled by the copy editor. But this is rare anymore, and most publishing houses put you, the author, in charge of getting permissions. This makes good sense because you know what you are using and what is going to require permission. So, in the course of your writing, you should be corresponding with publishers of copyrighted material and asking them for permission to reprint material in your book. And when you deliver your final manuscript to your editor, you need to send copies of the permissions letters you have obtained.

If you have not obtained the necessary permissions statements by the time you have finished your manuscript, you will be asked to move apace to secure the rights to the material. Most houses will allow you to secure the permissions while your manuscript is being edited and designed, but it must be done as quickly as possible. Publishers are most interested at this point in the *legal* ramifications for publishing already copyrighted material; they are not so much concerned with the *financial* arrangements. This is true because most publishing contracts state that permissions fees are to be taken care of by the author, and this is usually done out of future royalty earnings. But no publisher wants to lose time, energy, and money setting material in type only to find out that things need to be deleted because permissions cannot be obtained.

The Author's Questionnaire and Other Forms

By now you have probably been asked by your publisher to fill out an author's questionnaire form. If not, you will be asked to complete one. This long and sometimes complicated form, which provides much additional information about you, is needed by several people in different departments within the publishing house—not only the editorial department but also the various promotional departments, including sales, marketing, advertising, and publicity. Any other forms that a particular house uses will be sent to you and completed at this stage also.

It's important to spend some quality time on these forms. No one much likes filling them out, but keep in mind that they are helpful to a number of people whose job is to help you. Don't be a prima donna author who says, "My job is to write the book, and your job is to write the blurbs, cover copy, author information, and so on." That is an unhelpful attitude.

Transmittal and Copyediting

Now that the substantive editing has been done and the rights and permissions taken care of, the sponsoring or acquiring editor sends the manuscript over to the copyediting and production department. This is when the sponsoring editor goes over with the copy editor whatever original evaluation he or she has gathered and what they think needs to be done with the material, including the sort of copyediting it requires. At this stage, a line-by-line editing is done on the manuscript. The editing could be a light one, a heavy one, or one that is substantial enough to be considered an overhaul or rewrite.

What is the copy editor's task? It is to sit down and carefully read all of the manuscript, to reason about each line and paragraph of it. It is to check the entire typescript and to bring it into consistency with the house style. In other words, the copy editor enforces the mechanical conventions of style: spelling, grammar, punctuation, and so on, marking the manuscript so that the text will require a minimum of alterations after it is set into type. The good copy editor also looks for typographical errors, infelicities of style, errors of fact, and logical inconsistencies. He or she tries to catch the circular argument, the anachronism, or the potentially libelous remark. Copy editors do all of this because, with the rush of modern publishing programs, the copy editor may be the only one who really sits down and reads the manuscript line by line.

If something really serious is found during the copy-editing stage of the manuscript, the copy editor usually brings this to the attention of the sponsoring editor or the editorial director. When certain matters cannot be cared for by the editing staff, most often the author is queried. When a query list goes out to an author, this can be done piecemeal, chapter by chapter, or *en masse*. Sometimes when the query letter goes out, the edited manuscript also accompanies it. This is to show the author the proposed changes and to ask for the author's approval or disapproval—to see if the author agrees that the proposed changes improve the book. Whatever disagreements an author has with the copyediting of a manuscript ought to be mentioned at this point, and final changes should then be transferred to the manuscript.

The edited manuscript does not always go back to the author, however. The reason for this is because many copy editors now do their work on screen only, not on the actual manuscript itself. This means that when the author sees the changes, he will see them not made manually on the hard copy of the typescript but rather in the first set of page proofs. However an author sees the suggested manuscript changes, one thing all authors and editors ought to agree on is that the copyediting process is not supposed to be done by confrontation. In other words, no one is to change the author's intent because they do not like or agree with what the author says. That is a definite no-no, and it is really not professional editing.

Production and Design

After the material has been copyedited, it is then sent into the keeping of the people in the production area (or creative services or marketing, depending on the structure of the publishing house). Either at this stage, or sometimes before this stage during the review process, various decisions are made on the book—what it will look like, what it will cost, how it will be marketed and sold, and dozens of other considerations. Usually a committee of people from the appropriate departments will meet to decide things such as the design and format of the book, the sort of cover art that will be used, what binding the book will have, what the trim size will be, what list or retail price the book should sell for, what discounts will be offered to buyers, the nature and number of the first print run, what illustrations or artwork should be involved, what projected publication date makes sense, when the book will be introduced in the publisher's catalog and to the retail market, the method of printing, the type of paper, the size and style of typesetting, and various other manufacturing aspects. Whew! Many, many questions arise during the production and design stage in book publishing, and once all these questions are answered and the printing schedule is set up, the manuscript is launched.

The production department, or the marketing department, depending on the publishing house, is also the area most concerned with the content of the dust jacket or back cover copy of the book, as well as the catalog copy.

Usually while the copyediting is being accomplished, three other important things are going on at the same time in the art or production departments: interior design, preparation of camera-ready artwork, and cover design. Let's turn to each one.

Interior Design

The book designer is responsible for choosing the dimensions of the book in relation to the printed text—in other words, for choosing the technical specifications of the book. The work of the book designer guides the typesetter, the printer, the binder, and the cover artist. After reviewing a copy of the manuscript, and after being told by either the editorial department or the production department of the technical features of the book that have already been decided (such as the trim size, the type of binding, and the desired page length), the designer then marks the manuscript with type specifications and does ten or a dozen sample page layouts. These layouts are drawings of what the actual book pages will look like at actual page size.

Sample pages come next. After the designer has marked the manuscript, it is usual for the production supervisor to ask the typesetter for some sample pages just to see what the proposed design looks like. This is shown to the editorial department and others to see if everyone is satisfied that the design works. When everyone agrees the design is sound and the copyediting is complete, off the entire manuscript goes to the typesetter.

Preparation of Artwork

In bookmaking, the definition of *art* is a bit different from how art is viewed in most other contexts. In book publishing, art is anything that is not set in type. This could be charts, graphs, photographs (called "halftones"), diagrams (called "line art"), a table of figures, or even a diacritical mark over a letter in a foreign word. In book work, then, art is not defined by its content; it is defined by the technique that produces it. There are many refinements involving screens, second colors, overlays, and so forth, which most writers and editors don't begin to understand. The point is, however, if you have any illustrations of any kind in your book, now is the time the artists and graphic designers begin working on them. They do this by taking the author's "roughs" (whether pencil sketches or diagrams that have been borrowed or created), photos and illustrations, and redrawing them or sizing them so they can be rendered in camera-ready form. They also have to carefully check setting, placement, and accuracy of the captions that will appear below the artwork.

Where do these artists who specialize in books reside in the publishing house? They may be part of the production department or the marketing department. They may have a department of their own, and in large houses they usually do. In smaller houses often this kind of work is sent outside to firms that specialize in photo processing, key lining, pasteup, draftsmanship, and separation.

Cover Design and Jacket Copy

While all this production and interior design work has been taking place, the cover design has not been forgotten, for the development and design of the cover or book jacket goes on at the same time the text is being developed and edited. In fact, exterior or cover design receives as much or more attention from the various departments in a publishing house as just about anything else. What a book looks like physically is *very* important because it is the *exterior* of the book that bookstore buyers and readers see first. And of course all authors want their books to look attractive and appealing.

Many publishers do not allow authors to have any input whatsoever on the proposed book cover, preferring to leave the cover to experts in the field. Many houses will allow the author to see the proposed design, and maybe even to comment on it, but they do not allow the author any sort of veto power over it. Some authors who are more widely known and published are allowed a "mutual approval" consultation with the publisher on the proposed jacket design and flap copy. Only the best-known and highly influential authors are allowed to approve these things. But even for these few authors, this approval must be written into the contract. We do not advise most authors to expect or attempt to get this type of approval.

Covers are almost always done by artists or designers who specialize in book cover art, and the artist could be either a staff artist or a freelancer. They are given certain guidelines, including dimensions of the book such as the trim size and the copy to appear on the jacket, and they return sometime later with some proposed sketches on cover ideas that then have to be passed around and examined and approved or rejected by the art director and editorial director and others involved in the book. Often at this point sketches are sent to the author for reaction. Ultimately, the cover is refined so that everyone finds it satisfactory, possibly even the author.

Authors are justifiably concerned over not being allowed final approval of the cover design and copy. After all, it is their work that is being packaged and summed up on the cover or jacket, and it is a biography of their life that is summarized in a paragraph or two. But if an author simply provides, as completely and accurately as possible, all the autobiographical information and the other information that the publishing staff requests (in the author's questionnaire form), then the best we can hope for is that the information will be used in the best way possible.

In any event, before long copies of the approved cover are handed out to the field sales reps, so they can use them in the advance selling of the book. In many cases the salespeople are able to get finished covers well before the actual book appears from the press because the covers or the jackets usually are printed separately from the sheets that make up the book. They are printed on heavier paper and even on a different press. In this way, extra jackets or covers can be printed early enough for the sales reps to have them months before the book is finished, allowing them to promote the advance sales of the book.

You are now close to the end of the book production process, and you are also probably pretty close to the end of your rope. When all of this happens, your book has been born and is out in the open marketplace of ideas—maybe not to earn you piles of money but more importantly to strike a blow for the kingdom of God.

CHAPTER 9
The Relationship between Writers and Editors

Here is a story we told in our book *Inside Religious Publishing*. It is about the mighty dragon that lived in a cave on the side of a mountain high above a peace-loving village. Every day—sometimes all day—the mighty dragon would stand outside the cave and roar, with a roaring that could be heard far and wide. Looking up, the fearful people of the village saw the dragon brooding, glowering, and threatening, and they wrung their hands and were sad that they had to live in the shadow of this fearsome monster. It was no wonder that even the bravest people in the village were afraid.

Then one day, a certain small boy announced that he would go to fight the dragon. With great maturity, he said, "I will not live where fires cannot be lighted, where children do not go outside to play, and where men stay away from the fields because they live in fear.

"I will go and face the dragon," the boy proclaimed. And though the elders of the village and all his fellow villagers tried to dissuade him, he went. As the boy made his way up the mountain, he discovered a strange thing. The closer he came to the dragon's cave, the smaller the dragon seemed to be. At last when the boy arrived at the cave opening, the mighty dragon had become a creature so small that the boy could hold him in the palm of his hand. Whereupon our boy hero took the tiny monster and carried it back to the village.

Thus the mighty dragon turned out to be far less fearsome than once imagined. The tale of the mighty dragon is a parable of publishing, and it reveals what will happen when you become acquainted with this mysterious industry. For writers looking in from the outside, publishing may look like an awful dragon. You may think of publishers and the editors who work for them as monsters in the entrance to a cave. We want to assure you that editors are much like people in any other creative endeavor; they are not awful dragons, although some of them are little monsters.

What should the relationship be between writers and editors? How can we work together to contribute to the publishing enterprise, trying through Christian literature to communicate the gospel of Christ? Why is there an almost natural antagonism between editors and authors? What things should the editor and the author look for in each other? How do editors make their publishing decisions? These are the questions we would like to explore in this chapter.

Why We Publish

In many ways people in Christian publishing are like other people in book publishing, and they are in the book business for many of the same reasons. Some say it is because they love books. They enjoy the feel and even the smell of a new book. They feel the excitement a new book gives them when they sit down to read. Others are in publishing for a more pragmatic reason, or for the economic viewpoint; publishing for them is a job, a venture in selling and profits. Still others enter Christian publishing because of the ministry opportunities.

Whatever the motives for becoming involved in this field, one must stop and ask what this business is really about (this was the theme of our first chapter). Yes, we produce and promote books, and so that means we're in the "book business." A book is a product or commodity, with a cover, a binding, pages with ink on them, and a retail price. But isn't a book more than a mere commodity? Is that all there is? If you say yes to this, we want to suggest you think of some other area where you might more fruitfully spend your time than in writing books. But if you say no to this, if you think a book is far more than a mere commodity and that it is actually about promoting ideas, then you might be the sort of writer who can find a place in this field.

We quoted Saul Bellow in our preface, but we think his comment merits repeating here on the topic of why we publish. He said, "[There is] an immense, painful longing for a broader, more flexible, fuller, more coherent, more comprehensive account of what we human beings are, who we are, and what this life is for." That is why writers and editors ought to be in the Christian publishing business—to help our readers discover what this life is for.

Promoting Ideas

It isn't enough to keep the presses rolling. It isn't enough to love to read, to love books, or even to have an interest in some aspect of ministry. What must you have? You must have an unquenchable desire to get books and readers together. You have to be excited about communicating the ideas you have, or the ideas that are in your books, and what those ideas can do for your potential readers. Christian writing and Christian book publishing are about much more than mere bookselling. They are about promoting Kingdom-sized *ideas*.

Christian publishers need the same tools all other publishers need: a wide selection of authors; titles with logical and practical application for various readers; books with a high quality of writing, graphics, and production value; eye-catching covers; attractive store displays; market research; and so on. We need books that have a reason for being written in the first place. But Christian writers and Christian editors should also know that we need something more than all this. We need to know that *ideas catch fire*. Selling books is important, but promoting an *idea* begins a series of ripples that can go on forever.

Now admittedly, this is somewhat theoretical and imaginative. The reality in day-to-day publishing is sometimes quite different. Overcoming all the obstacles and details of book publishing, such as proofing the third and fourth galleys and getting out from under the piles of manuscripts and correspondence, can pretty much smother an editor's enthusiasm. By the time a book appears from the press, it is often more with a feeling of relief than triumph.

And then, when you really look into things, you discover that all this talk about books multiplying your influence a thousand times by putting words on paper—well, that can be mythological. What you mostly multiply is *words,* not influence. You find that people read pretty much what they already agree with, if they read at all. In other words, the influence writers and publishers have is real, but it is far less often than we might imagine.

If this is true, why should we publish? We believe it is because God has given us the gift of books. We publish them to please ourselves and others who, like us, love and want books. And we publish because Christians depend on books to build a deep foundation. Books have the depth to let thinkers develop their thoughts and engage in dialogue with others. They enable one generation to leave a heritage for the next. We feel the world needs the value of books. In short, we enjoy our association with books and ideas and with people who love books and ideas.

If you are reading this book, we assume you are a person who also loves books and ideas. Because you love these things, and because you want to write for publication, you need to know about a few things from the worlds of writing and publishing, including how authors and editors work together. Let's examine this subject.

Why the Conflict between Editors and Authors?

One editor once suggested that publishers have long been working on a machine that will replace the author as the greatest nuisance in publishing! This editor said so with his tongue in his cheek because he knows as everyone knows that we need authors. Publishing does not go on without writers. Still, there does seem at times to be a tendency for editors and authors to be hostile to each other. Could there be a good and even helpful reason for this? We think so.

Editor Ken Purdy, in Gerald Gross's book *Editors on Editing,* put it this way: "The relationship between the editor and the writer is, now and then, a happy one. Now and then, indeed. A warm, pleasant, long-standing relationship between an editor and a writer is a rarity. By the very nature of things it must be. These two people, the editor and the writer, do not begin to understand each other."

Is it a truism that editors and authors do not get on well together? Perhaps most would say it is. But *why* is this so, and why can't there be a happier relationship? In his book *The Elements of Editing,* Arthur Plotnik explains it this way:

> Editors need writers and have been known to end up liking a few. But editors are foot soldiers in the eternal war between raw talent and the people who process that talent. As long as writers write primarily to advance themselves and editors edit to satisfy readers, there will never be a lasting peace. An editor's only permanent alliance is with the audience, the readership. It is the editor's responsibility to *hook* that readership—to edify it, entertain it, stroke it, *shake it up*—to do whatever is necessary to keep the medium hot and desirable for the people who support it. The editor, not the author, best understands that

readership. Authors know their subject. Editors specialize in knowing the audience. . . . Because an editor's self-esteem and very job depend on satisfying readers, it is the *reader,* not the author, who will receive first consideration when conflicts of interest arise. A good editor will fight to the death even against the almighty publisher if readers are being abused.[1]

What Plotnik is saying is that when push comes to shove, the editor is not on the side of the writer but on the side of the reader. And this accounts for the almost natural antagonism between editors and writers. Whatever we make of this, one thing is sure: there would be no editors without writers. As more than one Christian editor has said, "Writers are our bread and butter even if they are sometimes the bane of our existence!"

What Editors Look for in Writers

Writing would certainly continue without editors and editing, and even without publishing. But as the converse is not true, editors are always looking for writers. What do editors look for in writers? They are looking for writers who are reasonably professional. We put it this way because of the editorial role itself. It is the role of guide rather than teacher. The reason editors should not operate as teachers is twofold. First, this is due to economic necessity. When you consider the number of manuscripts a publishing house deals with, even at a small house you will realize that a single editor cannot spend a great deal of time with each manuscript. A single editor works with many manuscripts at one time and simply doesn't have the time necessary to teach every author all there is to know about the writing craft.

The second reason editors should not be thought of as teachers is that writers typically are better writers than editors. Many editors are fine writers, but for the most part writers are far better at the job of writing than editors. Writers are the creative bunch. Editors are more interested in the technical aspects of the words on the page, not necessarily the creative aspect of writing itself. Writers know their subject, and they know how best to write about that subject. Editors know the reading audience, and they try to hone written material to that audience.

For these two reasons you can see why editors are looking for reasonably professional writers who already know the craft of writing. But what do editors do when they get a reasonably professional manuscript from a reasonably professional writer? This is anybody's guess.

The Editor's Job

Every book editor works in a different way. Some approach their work as an art, or at least that's how they express the work of the editor. Others say that editing is more in the nature of a science. Some regard it as a craft. One of our authors has worked as a book editor for twenty-five years. To him editing is not so much an art, a science, or a craft but a crusade! The point is that editors are all different, and each approaches the editorial function individually. But this much we can say: all editors are paid to process words into communication packages.

There are no hard and fast rules about being a book editor. It is merely a matter of style. Each is different, and each works in his or her own way. Editors recognize that authors are different individuals, and each one must be dealt with in an individual way. In the same way you as an author need to know that you should deal with each editor in a unique way. The only way editors can determine how to deal with any particular author is to begin working with that author and see how things go. We suppose it is the same for authors dealing with editors.

While the approach to editorial *work* is varied, the editorial *function* can be simply put, and it is threefold: the editor must find manuscripts, develop manuscripts, and sell the manuscripts to the in-house selling departments, including the sales force, the publicity and marketing departments, and the publisher who ultimately spends all the money. The editor's job is to get the right idea together with the right author. Never mind where the idea came from. It could be an idea from the author, suggesting they work on this or that particular project. It might be the editor's idea, which he or she then farms out to a writer. But ultimately, the rubber meets the road when we get the right idea in the hands of the right author. Get this mix right, and you've got a winning book.

Whatever else editors do, they find the best manuscripts they can find (from reasonably professional writers), develop manuscripts and hone them for the specified audience, and guide writers while they are developing their writing projects. Another thing editors do is haunt the halls of the publishing house in order to sell projects to the people inside the house who promote the book outside. In book publishing everything happens in the halls, and editors spend a lot of time in the corridors trying to get others enthusiastic about the great projects they are working on.

If writers feel, as most editors do, that the key to the success of any book lies as much in the editorial and publishing process as in the process of its creation, then they have a high view of editing. But this does not mean they understand all the things that go on behind the editorial scenes regarding how editorial decisions are made. Some of our readers are experienced writers, yet even experienced writers sometimes wonder about the person who handles the material they submit to a publisher. Previously unpublished writers certainly do. Let's take a closer look.

How Editorial Decisions Are Made

Most writers probably think that after they have put part of their lives into a writing project, and painstakingly shipped it off to a carefully chosen publishing house, that someone, somewhere, with some set of objective criteria, will weigh their effort and arrive at some professional assessment of whether it is in acceptable shape and ready to be published. But all too often this is not the case. Publishing is an incredibly arbitrary business, and a lot of great manuscripts get by editors or don't make it through the publishing committee process. Why?

Consider the plight of the poor editor. There she sits, alone in her office. Piled high on the office book shelves and all over the floor are dozens of manuscripts, most of which have never been solicited. Out of this entire "slush pile" (unsolicited manuscripts that pile up at a publishing house), perhaps only a few appear at first blush to have any promise. And the editor isn't sure what to do about *those*. She hates to turn down anything that has a spark of talent or some merit. Her future depends on *discovering* books, not returning manuscripts. And so some editors allow themselves to become paralyzed in the decision-making process, not wanting to turn down a book for fear they are making a big mistake, for fear someone else might get it, for fear it might become a bestseller. The editor is afraid of her own judgment and afraid of buying too many books that cost but do not pay.

Every editor makes mistakes, and on occasion most of them would be willing to regale writers with stories of the humongous mistakes they've made. But if turning down a publishable manuscript is a mistake, then publishing a manuscript that should have been rejected is an even bigger mistake. This is another way of saying that we in Christian publishing have produced far too many books that probably should never have been published. The idea is to keep from publishing more of those kinds of projects.

Therefore, to keep from being paralyzed in the decision-making process, editors must learn to make editorial decisions quickly, sharply, and without regret. Otherwise, they spend almost all their time reading manuscripts that may not be worth reading, let alone publishing. The most common editorial activity is saying no, and someone with editorial judgment has to do it. Some people say that editors are the "priests" of the publishing house because they sometimes have the first and final vote on a manuscript. As such, publishing decisions often begin and end with the editor. And this is true in most publishing companies.

Because entire publishing programs are in the hands of editors, editorial workers must guard how they spend their time, learning how to spend it wisely and well. There are many things an editor can do, even good things, but there is not enough time for everything. There isn't even enough time for all the *good* things, so the editor must attempt to do all the *best* things. They must guard against substituting the good for the best. And this, most editors would say, has been the flaw in Christian publishing. We have published a good many things that probably should not have been published. Now it's time to turn our attention to the *best* things. It's time to tell writers to give us your very best and only your very best. Remember God's words to Moses in Numbers 18: "Give it from the best that you receive" (TEV).

In the final analysis, most titles added to a publisher's list are accepted on the basis of a subjective reaction, which is at times quite arbitrary.

Five Points on the Author and Editor Relationship

What should an author expect from the editor? We want to suggest at least five things. First, the author ought to look to the editor for help in focusing on the audience. Every editor has received dozens of manuscripts from writers saying, "This manuscript is for everyone. Everyone will want to read this." That is never true, so don't say it. No writer has an audience with the entire world in general. Books are written to specific groups, and no book has a universal readership. Authors should know that editors can help direct the material toward the specific or intended reading target; indeed, this is the specialty of the editor. In the editor's mind, the audience for a book or article is the first and prime importance, so look to the editor for understanding and focusing on the audience.

Second, the author ought to look to the editor for the writing deadline. Many writers wonder why they should look to editors for something that seems to curtail their creativity. But the deadline should be regarded in a higher light than it usually is, and you should be grateful to have one. The reason for this is that, for most writers, the deadline is the motivation to productivity. Otherwise, material would never be completed and submitted. Writers need a prod. The author Wayne Oates used to say the deadline is "a mobilizer of anxieties," and this is certainly true; it is a clarifier of one's thinking.

In an interview with the University of Chicago theologian, church historian, and prolific author Martin Marty, the interviewer asked, "How do you get all your work done?" Marty responded this way: "Deadlines is my usual answer and the most true. It's not the only one, but that's basically it. I am going through life never having written a book or article that I have said, 'I think I'll write.' I've always responded to assignments, and assignments come with deadlines. That's a marvelous discipline."

Third, authors should look to editors for answers having to do with the book's editorial and production schedule. Usually, the answers the author has in mind have to do with book manufacturing, sales, and marketing. Most of the time, however, the editor doesn't have the answers, and this is because while the author has but one book in mind, the editor has lots of books in mind at any one time. Sometimes authors contact editors about every little detail regarding the progress of a book. They get angry when the editor doesn't have all the answers immediately at hand.

Again, that is because the author's book is not the only one the editor is working on. Experienced, published writers know that editorial and publishing work cannot be rushed. It is the mark of the amateur to think that everything has to be done quickly. The amateur has what Charlie Shedd called "a serious case of the hurry-ups."

Things take time in publishing, and even getting answers takes time. But usually, the editor is the author's main contact person for a given project, and it is the editor's responsibility to try to keep abreast of the book— where it is in editorial and manufacturing production, how it is doing in sales, where it will be advertised, where it has been sent out for reviews, when it will appear in the catalog, and so on.

Fourth, the author should look to the editor for creativity and style. This has to do not only with broad topics but with how the topic itself is handled. In other words, what *style* should the material take, and what amount of editing work should be done on a manuscript? With more academic or technical titles, an editor almost never deals with a professional writer. These writers obviously are specialists in other fields, and for this reason editors on the whole do more work on these kinds of manuscripts. But even nontechnical works can require editing, sometimes extensive editing or even a good deal of rewriting. When this is done, many writers become unhappy.

Why? The reason for this is obvious and understandable, for as far as the author is concerned, the manuscript is more than a mere manuscript; it is a part of that author's life. It is almost another pair of hands, and with each change the editor makes, the nails are trimmed.

With additional changes, the tips of the fingers are cut off. Then go the rest of the fingers, and after that, maybe the whole hand! Authors know that what editors edit is far more than just manuscripts: it is part of their lives. Therefore, authors get angry with editors for too many changes, even when they know the changes are absolutely necessary.

We suggest authors try to control the prima donna attitude that "God told me to say that, so you can't change it!" Too many Christian writers have the notion that inspired writing is writing directly inspired by God, which therefore requires no editing. Now God *does* inspire writers with many wonderful, creative ideas. Most editors have seen this divine creative nudge many times. But this does not negate the necessity to edit and rewrite serious work. If your work has been inspired by God, then you should handle it as a sacred trust, polishing it to a fine edge. Don't just turn it in saying it's from God's own mouth because nobody will buy that. You may think that published, professional writers do not display this prima donna attitude, but it happens all the time, and it is easy to understand why. Success spoils appreciation of the editing process. Some writers think, *Why should I let the editor change my words when my words appear to be worth so much?* The truth is, no matter how good or successful a writer you are, God is not looking for a stenographer to take down his words, and he has not given you any miraculous ability in writing.

Success brings with it the temptation to congratulate ourselves. Then we begin making our own rules. Taking exceptions to the old standards, we forsake our roots. Just remember that the higher you go in the writing career

God has given you, the more time you should spend on your knees. Don't ever forget to refer your success to the Source of that success, and then get rid of any prima donna inclinations, for they can't possibly help you in the long run.

What would you do if you were an editor receiving a letter like this? "Dear Editor, God gave me every word of this story, so I know it's good. I realize it is different, but I can assure you it is directly from God. I just want you to know, too, God told me to send this manuscript to you. He told me you were the one he chose to publish it. Sincerely yours, Inspired Writer." If you were the editor receiving such a note, and every editor worth his or her salt has received many such notes, you might want to respond this way: "Dear Inspired Writer, I'm returning this manuscript to you. Until I hear directly from God about publishing it, I'll pass. Sincerely yours, the Editor."

Remember also that what usually attracts an editor to a raw manuscript is not perfection. After all, no one has ever seen a perfect manuscript. Rather, what attracts an editor is the *potential* a manuscript has for being shaped into a successful book. Many successfully published books were not worth much as raw manuscripts. In any event, look to your editor on matters of style.

Fifth, the author should look to the editor for suggestions on rewrite. Rewriting is one of the author's bloodiest disciplines, and no one cares for it very much. But at times, material needs extensive rewriting. Remember this epigram: "Most people can write, but only writers can rewrite." Good writing is in fact mostly rewriting. Anthony Burgess said he might revise a single page as many as twenty times. Short story writer Road Dahl said by the time he neared the end of a story, the first part would have been reread and corrected as many as one hundred and fifty times. Ernest Hemingway said he rewrote the final chapter of *A Farewell to Arms* thirty-nine times.

Mark Twain was right to say that "writing is easy. All you have to do is cross out the wrong words." Close enough is not good enough. Our duty is to make ourselves fully understood. Good writing, which usually requires serious rewriting, will get you further than average writing in the long run. Our ego is safe when we have to rewrite, and only real writers care enough to continue grappling with their words to get the best out of themselves.

Your editor may ask you to rewrite portions of your manuscript, even if you've published several books. You won't like the thought, but recall the words of Alistair Cooke, who said, "A professional is a person who can do his best work when he doesn't feel like it." Good writers are seldom satisfied with their first efforts, and the success of any writer is in direct ratio to the number of times that writer goes back to write.

Notes

1. Arthur Plotnik, *The Elements of Editing* (New York: MacMillan Publishing Company, 1996).

CHAPTER 10

Trends in Christian Publishing: Agents, Conferences, Fiction, and Other New Phenomena

Life is never static but is constantly changing. That is especially true with Christian publishing. Many changes have occurred over the past two decades that seem to be moving publishing in areas never before imagined. When your authors, Len and Don, began writing and editing in the 1970s (yes, we really are that old!), a relatively small number of companies specialized in Christian publishing; a few well-known authors dominated the field; and, in general, changes seemed to come slowly to this segment of publishing. Has that changed today!

More companies are getting into the religious/inspirational field, and the general population has developed an appetite for the fare these companies serve up. Authors are achieving crossover status; that is, they sell well in both the religious and the general markets. An example is

Rick Warren's book, *The Purpose Driven Life*. Over twenty million copies have been purchased by people active in churches and by the nonchurched populace who are nevertheless searching for meaning in their lives. Another example is Joel Osteen's *Your Best Life Now*, which sold an incredible three million copies and is still going strong. The *Left Behind* fiction phenomenon authored by Jerry Jenkins and Tim LaHaye has left behind the competition by selling over sixty million copies!

New companies are starting up to focus on Christian publishing, and established businesses are starting new divisions or buying established houses to reach the religious reader. For example, Time-Warner began a new division, Warner Faith, located in Nashville. They publish Osteen's book.

In this chapter we want to introduce some of the current changes and trends so writers can realize what they are up against and how to position themselves for successful careers. We understand fully that God leads people to work in this industry, both as writers and as publishers, and with God's help anything can happen. But we also know that the more a writer learns and develops his or her skills, the better opportunity that writer will have when doors finally open. In other words, plan now for success later.

Agents

One of the fairly recent trends in Christian publishing is the work of agents. An agent is simply a middleman between the writer and the publisher. The agent's job is to help the writer find just the right publisher and then to work out a contract that will benefit the writer. General publishing has used agents for many years, but their use in Christian publishing is a new development. Chuck Swindoll used an agent in 1989 to negotiate a forty-five-title, ten-year contract with Word. Since then, agents have been increasingly visible in Christian circles. Some top authors, with the help of savvy agents, are now negotiating multimillion-dollar deals with publishers.

Not every writer who teams up with an agent will see those figures, of course. But agents are here to stay whether publishers like it or not. Agent Steve Laube quotes David Lindsey who, in his book *Rules of Silence,* says this about agents: "The literary agent toils at a mysterious alchemy, impossibly combining words and dollars in the ever-hopeful pursuit of forging the bright ore of a writing career that will serve to the mutual benefit of all the parties involved. It is an enigmatic profession involving a complex brew of relationships among author and agent and publisher and public."

We asked several editors to comment on their working relationships with agents. Their opinions vary from enthusiastic to reluctant acceptance.

Ted Griffin, senior editor at Crossway Books, has this view. "We work with agents, generally those who are known in the Christian publishing industry. This is sometimes beneficial, sometimes troubling. Agents are playing more and more of a major role in the industry. This is not always a good thing; some focus too much on the financial aspects of the relationship between an author and publisher."

For Gary Terashita, former Broadman & Holman editor and now with Warner Faith, the relationship with agents can be different depending on the person involved: "I work with agents, and experiences have ranged from helpful to downright depressing. The primary role played by agents in our industry is connecting authors with publishers."

Andy LePeau at IVP has much to say about agents and their role in publishing today. "We work with agents some. Most agents don't work with authors or books that fit IVP, more thoughtful stuff. But some do. We probably work with them less than many publishers who are oriented to the CBA audience/market.

"Generally I think we are neutral on agents. They have some plusses and minuses. An agent can help an author have realistic expectations of a publisher or see the value of the publisher's experience regarding what title works or doesn't work."

While the relationship between an agent and an author should be one of mutual support, the relationship between agent and publisher is also one of respect and mutual benefit. LePeau says, "To some extent I think it is a myth that agents are more neutral or more pro-author than a publisher. Somehow the idea is that publishers are only out for the money and agents are only out for the author. I don't know why that should be so. After all, agents have their own financial interests in mind as well! Ideally, publishers should give just as much care and attention to their authors and manuscripts as the agents do, if not more so."

Given the rise of the agent in Christian publishing, does that function always help produce a better book? Are Christian agents better than, or even as good as, their secular counterparts? LePeau says of his experience,

"Sometimes I find secular agents much more professional and reasonable to deal with than Christian agents. There are exceptions both ways, of course."

Chip MacGregor, formerly with Alive Communications Inc., one of the largest and most influential agencies representing Christian authors, helps to explain how the publishing process looks from the agent's viewpoint. He says:

> Most publishers, including most Christian publishers, simply do their business through agents. Publishing houses rely on agents to do the initial weeding so that the proposals being considered by acquisitions editors have already been vetted in some way. The dross has been skimmed away. Agents (at least reputable agents) have the relationships in place to get your proposal seen by the right people—something many beginning writers lack. They also understand publishing contracts, so they can protect you from making a bad decision—an important but often overlooked point, since the document you sign is a legal agreement that will govern the terms of your writing for the life of the project. And a good agent will know the market so that he or she can negotiate a contract on your behalf that is in line with current market standards.

> Most importantly, an agent can offer you direction and advice to help you shape your writing career, and I can think of few other sources to whom a writer can turn for that type of

help. (While I love publishers, I don't think they make great career counselors. A publishing house is concerned, first and foremost, with the success of the publishing house, not the long-term success of any individual author.) Therefore, in many ways the agent becomes the go-between, working with both authors and publishers to identify good ideas, foster great writing, negotiate a deal that works for both sides, and ensure the long-term future of the author. But remember that your agent works for you, not for the publisher. Your agent ought to be singing your praises, assisting you in the process, and looking out for your best interests.

MacGregor realizes that life in general is getting more complicated. An agent can help cut through some of the complexity on behalf of an author and allow that writer to focus on the creative process. He says:

Though some Christian publishers still take a fairly paternalistic attitude toward authors, and seem to resent the intrusion of agents into their small, controlled world, the fact is that every professional genre moves toward more specialization, and therefore needs people who are experts in the fine print. For example, selling a home used to be a fairly easy transaction to undertake. You turned over some cash, you signed an agreement, and the deal was done. That's still the basic premise of a home sale today; but with various commissions, layers of government, and everybody from insurance

offices to title companies trying to get a piece of
the deal, it's become considerably more complex.
When my wife and I purchased our current home,
we spent nearly two hours in an office, signing
our names to nearly forty documents. You can
still sell a home on your own in this country; it's
just considerably harder than it used to be, and
it's going to take some significant learning on
your part to make sure it all gets done properly.
The same is true with a book deal. You can learn
a lot of the process and invest in the relationships
you're going to need, but you should know going
in that you're facing an uphill climb.

MacGregor adds two additional comments about
agents and their work in today's publishing environment.

First, not every author is a fit with every
agent. Sometimes, even two talented and friendly
people will be terrible business partners. So don't
be quick to sign with an agent. Check him or her
out, asking questions like: "Who do you
represent? Who have you done deals with? How
many deals have you done lately?" Different
agents, like different authors, will have unique
strengths. If you need an agent who can offer an
editorial eye, don't sign with one who is strong on
marketing but knows nothing about words. If you
need someone to handle all your business
arrangements, don't assume you'll be happy with
an agent whose strength is editing and discussing
ideas. Think carefully about what your
expectations are in an agent before signing any
sort of representation agreement.

Second, I know few good agents. Anybody can call themselves an agent these days, and I keep running into people calling themselves agents who don't know words, don't have strong publishing relationships, and don't know how to shape a writer's career. So, though you'll be tempted to sign with the first agent who expresses an interest in your work, be willing to take the long view.

Deidre Knight, founder of The Knight Agency in Atlanta, realizes that agents can help writers, especially beginners, avoid mistakes that can severely cripple their work. Knight says: "Beginning writers tend to attempt publication too early in their writing endeavors. They query about a first draft—or even an incomplete draft—of a work or proposal. In the past year the number one thing I've come back to for all writers is *slow down*. Read over the manuscript one more time, take it one level deeper, or give your agent a bit more time to market your material. Whatever area of your career, take a breath and slow down some. So in short, I see beginners rushing things too much, at all stages of the process."

The publishing environments are different between the general American Booksellers Association (ABA) and the Christian Booksellers Association (CBA). Knight says of beginning writers, "I think writers have an excellent chance of being published, though it certainly helps to have an agent, particularly in ABA where it rarely happens otherwise. In CBA a writer can certainly still find publication without an agent, but I think more and more it's a help to have that intermediary who already has established relationships with the various publishing houses."

Steve Laube operates his own agency but has seen several sides of the Christian publishing arena. He has been the manager of a bookstore, the editor at a large publishing house, and worked for a large secular agency before opening his agency. When asked what he brings to the table to benefit both the writer and publisher, Laube points to the content of his Web site:

Our service philosophy can be described in three words.

1. Content: To help the author develop and create the best book possible. Material that has both commercial appeal and long-term value.

2. Career: To help the author determine the next best step in their writing career. Giving counsel regarding the subtleties of the marketplace as well as the realities of the publishing community.

3. Contract: To help the author secure the best possible contract. One that partners with the best strategic publisher and one that is mutually beneficial for all parties involved.

Laube has seen the role of agents change dramatically in Christian publishing. He observes: "The role of the agent in CBA has grown and matured considerably in the last few years. Gone are the days where there were only a couple good writers and a couple good publishers. Fiction had a half dozen authors at best and A. W. Tozer and *Strong's Concordance* resided on the best-sellers list. Now we have hundreds of talented people who have been given the gift of communication. And while authors have become more adept, publishers have become more professional."

That fact raises the issue of agents. Laube continues:

> In comes the agent question. Do you really need an agent? Does John Grisham or Stephen King need an agent? (Those fellows could offer their grocery list and secure a contract.) My answer is yes, depending on the scope of your writing and the nature of your connections in the publishing industry. One publisher recently told me that if they found a manuscript they wanted that was unagented they would tell the author to go get one and suggest a few names. They prefer to work with a known entity, someone they have worked with before. I had the same experience when I was with Bethany House. I wrote dozens of contracts with agents and dozens with the individual. It was clear that the agent knew what to ask for and the author did not. It was clear the agent knew what not to challenge and that the authors, many times, did not. With many agencies the contract became a fairly easy exercise because all the little idiosyncrasies of the contract had already been hashed out and did not need to be repeated on the next deal.

Laube notes that while having an agent can be beneficial to writers, actually getting one to represent a beginner is often difficult. He says, "As an agency we represent less than 1 percent of the authors who contact us. Nearly every client we represent we are able to get published and would like to keep that success rate. It is hard to get selected by a major house, but it still happens."

We asked the writers who offered their advice in chapters 3 and 4 about agents and their experiences. Here are the perspectives of working writers that represent their best judgment on the subject.

Alan Maki said:

> Many recommend agents. I used an agent in New York to get a three-book deal for me from Random House. All of the books were about Navy SEALs in Vietnam. I was negotiating a one-book deal, but the agent knew the editor and told me he could triple the deal if I used him. So in that case an agent was helpful.

> For my two Christian novels, I did not use an agent. I sent out a proposal with sample chapters, which ended up in the slush pile at Broadman & Holman Publishers, and fourteen weeks later I had a contract. That was the harder route to go, but the story was beautiful (if I may say so myself!) and fit a need at B&H. Without an agent, I had to overcome the obstacle (only 2 percent get published) and get a bit lucky. Bottom line: if a good agent wants to represent you, go for it. Otherwise, you're on your own, and you had better be really good.

Jan Coleman likes working through an agent because it frees her to do what she prefers doing, namely, writing.

> I finally got an agent after securing my first book contract and two work-for-hire projects myself. I want to spend my time writing and let

the agent handle knocking on publisher's doors. So many publishers don't want to see unsolicited manuscripts anymore, and unless you can go to a few big conferences a year to meet editors, it's hard to break in. I know authors who still don't have agents and don't want one, but they are few. My agent shops my books and deciphers the contracts; that's what I pay her for.

Stephen Clark observes: "I do not use an agent and am unsure what advantage there would be to use one at this time. That could change. It seems that more and more book publishers require authors approach them through agents, which is a big shift from a few years ago. They seem to be playing a more significant role in Christian publishing."

Susan Titus Osborn realizes that for her, using an agent would interfere with her relationships with editors built up over long years of ongoing contact. "I do not have an agent. I know everyone in the publishing industry and enjoy the personal contact with editors. An agent works well for those who are actively publishing who don't want to negotiate their contracts or don't have the time or desire to market their work." Osborn points out the difficulty of securing the services of an agent. "A new author can't get a good agent though, and a mediocre one will cause more harm than good. You need a proven track record before you seek an agent."

Ted Baehr has personal experience with one of the agents quoted in this book. When asked if he uses an agent, Baehr says, "Yes, I use an agent, Chip MacGregor, who is excellent. He opens doors, helps me to get better deals, and keeps me on track." That is probably about as succinct a description of an agent's work as you will see anywhere.

Vicki Caruana describes her reason for using an agent, namely, the agent can do things the writer would rather not do. "I use an agent. I have found that I don't handle the business end of writing very well. It's not a matter of whether I can get my work seen; it's a matter of my agent's handling the details and the problems that inevitably arise. I get easily distracted when things go wrong, and my agent is good at protecting me from those distractions. My agent is also my greatest cheerleader and someone who helps me plan out my writing career."

Some writers realize that the relationship with agents does not progress or grow as hoped. Ken Walker has a realistic view of this relationship. He says:

> I have had an agent twice. My first one dropped out of the business a few months after I signed an agreement with him, and I went for nearly two years without an agent—and also didn't have any book sales in the interim. I signed an agreement with my current agent after meeting him at a writers conference (another reason to go to conferences) in 2000. At the time I had been trying for nearly a year to sell a book I had coauthored. It took him another year before we had an agreement, but during that time one publisher was close to making an offer before backing away. Despite that disappointment he found another publisher who offered a contract.

My agent takes care of two primary things I hate: shopping book proposals and negotiating contracts. I'm not good at either one of them; and with more and more publishers only wanting to deal with agents, it makes sense to have one. Of course, if you're just a beginner, you don't need an agent. Agents don't negotiate magazine article sales, so you're on your own there anyway. And you're not likely to find an agent for a first-time book project but through showing a sample chapter to an editor at a writers conference or getting the editor to agree to look at a proposal after the conference ends.

Cecil Murphey has Deidre Knight, quoted above, as his agent. After having so-so relationships with several other agents before teaming with Knight, Murphey understands the ins and outs of the relationship.

I have had an agent since 1989 or 1990; I was one of the first Christian writers to sign with one. I changed agents in late 1996 and have been with my present agent since 1997. Good agents know what editors are looking for. They're more in touch with publishing trends and needs.

Agents can negotiate. That's important because I'm a wimp when it comes to negotiation. I did my own marketing of books before I went to an agent and learned a great deal about the business. It takes a lot of time and energy, both of which I'd prefer to put into my writing.

Good agents also help writers think ahead. "Where do you want to be in a year? In five

years?" I've written in areas I never thought
I would or could attempt because my agent said,
"You can do it."

Good agents are also cheerleaders. They turn
down most people who want representation and
sign only those that will earn them money. I feel
incredibly blessed to have such a great agent;
I know she's always out there pulling for me.

Janet Kobobel Grant, a well-known agent representing
Christian writers, aptly sums up the challenges and the
rewards of the writing life: "Moving from being a writer to
a successful author is a challenging, exciting, arduous,
fulfilling, frustrating, and ever surprising venture. Having
a good agent to travel with you down this path only
enriches the experience."

OK, so you are convinced that you should contact
an agent and see if you can find one to represent you.
Where do you begin? We suggest that you consult one
of the most helpful books any writer can own—
Sally Stuart's *Christian Writers Market Guide*. Her book,
which is updated annually, has a listing of agents who
represent Christian writers. Her Web site has several
links for agents: www.stuartmarket.com. You can also do
an Internet search for agents and find a plethora of information. But be cautious—some agents are really sharks
who charge upfront fees and deliver nothing. Carefully
check out anyone who ultimately offers to represent you.

Conferences

For many years beginning writers learned their skills
from two primary places: trial-and-error efforts and

attending one of the few national writers conferences for Christians. Until two decades ago, only a handful of these conferences existed. The Billy Graham organization hosted a national conference, as did Wheaton College and fewer than a dozen other organizations. The writer who wanted to attend one of those conferences usually had to reserve a week in the year, pay hundreds of dollars in fees, travel costs, and lodging.

All that began to change in the 1980s. Some of the large national conferences folded. In their place smaller regional conferences sprang up. Some large, nationally focused conferences still exist. You can find them listed in Sally Stuart's market book mentioned earlier. But many writers have found that attending a smaller, regionally focused conference is more efficient in both monetary and time expenditures. Instead of spending a full week and a thousand dollars at a conference, writers could attend for as little as one day for less than a hundred dollars.

One person who has helped revolutionize this regional concept is Reg Forder, publisher of *Christian Communicator* magazine and host of regional conferences under his American Christian Writers business umbrella. He has as many as thirty conferences each year in various cities around the country. His philosophy is that everyone should have access to a conference, even if just for one or two days. We asked Reg to explain his motivation for hosting the conferences and his philosophy of teaching.

Back in 1988 when we started hosting
Christian writers conferences around the country,
few others were offered. We instantly doubled and

later tripled the number of such conferences available to writers and would-be writers. Most of the writers at that time had never been to a Christian writers conference.

Of course, when we started hosting writing seminars in most of the major US cities, it quickly and substantially increased the number of writers seeking publication. That greatly increased the competition among writers, but it also resulted in raising the bar of quality in Christian writing. That was something we all wanted to see.

Over the years, in part because of increasing costs, several publishers have either gone out of business or merged with other more stable publishers. That and the fact that most book publishers have reduced the number of books published annually has made it more difficult for the new writer to find publication. A similar thing has happened in the Christian magazine industry. Several magazines have gone out of business, and others have reduced the number of issues published each year. All of this results in less opportunity for the writer.

Before this begins to sound too negative, I want to be quick to say the serious writer still has a good chance of being published. It may be that a smaller percentage of all writers are being published now, but I know that the people who are being regularly published are the ones who approach the craft seriously. They attend the conferences, read the books, study the market guides.

Another change that has taken place over these years is the increase of literary agents active in the Christian publishing world. The CBA has not yet got to the point it is in the ABA, but it is rapidly going that way. In a few years it may be near impossible to be published in CBA without the agent.

Forder has had the opportunity to meet hundreds of both successful writers and beginners through the years. He noticed that one factor above all separates the successful from the unsuccessful writers: "Probably the number one characteristic is 'persistence.' Only those committed to the craft succeed. And their goal must be something other than financial gain or fame. The number one reason beginning writers fail in this business is that they simply gave up too soon."

Forder has a ready answer when asked why writers should attend a conference. He notes, "With the increased competition today, there has never been a time when it has been more important to network with other people in the Christian publishing industry. In this business it isn't as much 'what you know' as it is 'who you know.' Beginning writers must meet other successful writers and editors to get a foot in the door of the publisher." Overall, the sky is the limit in the influence writers can have. "The opportunity to impact lives through our writing has never been greater. People are hungry for answers. The role of Christian publishing is more important today than at any time in the past. This and future generations need what we can provide for them."

Information on the American Christian Writers' Conferences are on the Internet at www.ACWriters.com.

Conferences are usually planned one to two years ahead, giving would-be participants plenty of lead time if they want to attend.

Lin Johnson is another conference director, writer, and editor. She heads up the well-known "Write-to-Publish" conference held each year in the Chicago area and also serves as the managing editor of *Christian Communicator* magazine and *Advanced Christian Writer.*

Johnson realizes that conferences can give beginning writers an edge in both content knowledge and personal contacts. She says, "Although writers can learn the craft of writing from books and tapes, conferences give them the opportunity to meet editors face-to-face and discuss their manuscripts with them. This kind of networking is invaluable. With more and more book houses not taking proposals through the mail, book authors need to meet editors at conferences to sell their books (or get agents, but they need to prove they can sell before most agents want to talk with them). The networking with writers is also valuable for encouragement and exchange of writing opportunities."

When asked how a person can get the most from a conference, Johnson has this advice:

> Go with a teachable spirit, and be open to God's leading. What you want to happen at a conference may not happen, but God has something else in mind for you.

> Carefully study the list of faculty and the program. Decide in advance whom you want to make appointments with, and prioritize that list in case you can't get the ones you want. Be

prepared to tell about your manuscript in one sentence, then expand on that description if an editor is interested. Eat with editors you can't get appointments with, talk with them between sessions, offer to pick them up or take them to the airport if you live in the area for more opportunities to get acquainted and pitch your manuscripts.

Further, Johnson urges conferees to think ahead about what they really need to learn to push their writing skills forward. She says:

Choose classes to hone your skills and expand your knowledge. Go to a class on a genre or topic that you know nothing about to see if you can expand your markets. Be sure to attend any editor panels. That's where you'll get a better idea of whether your writing will fit with specific houses/publications and often hear early announcements of changes at houses. If you can submit manuscripts for evaluation/critique, do so. The person in charge of manuscripts will match yours with the best faculty member. I've seen a number of book contracts come from this process.

But is going through all the trouble to attend a conference worth the effort and expense? Johnson's passion about the subject comes through clearly. "The best thing you can do for your writing career is to attend at least one writers' conference a year. Budget the time and money as part of your continuing education. In today's market conferences are no longer an option for writers who want to get published." Information on the Write-to-Publish conference hosted by Johnson can be found at her Web site: www.writetopublish.com.

Today's beginning writers are blessed with the abundance of choices regarding conferences. One or more are held in virtually every state. Some are in luscious settings, like the Glorieta, New Mexico, conference sponsored by CLASS (www.glorietacwc.com). Others are hosted by well-known writers, like the conference that Jerry Jenkins and his Christian Writers Guild puts on each year (www.ChristianWritersGuild.com). Some conferences take advantage of weather, like the Florida Christian Writers Conference held each spring (www.flwriters.org). Still others carry on a long tradition based at a college, such as the Write-to-Publish conference mentioned above. This list is only a *tiny* portion of conferences available. Check below for information on how to locate a conference that seems to match your needs.

Laraine Baxter, with Evangelical Christian Publishers Association (ECPA), a trade association for Christian publishers, advises all would-be writers to find one or more conferences to attend. "Attend writers conferences. I can't stress that enough. Attend larger ones where editors and published authors are in attendance." She advises writers to have their writing critiqued, even if that process is uncomfortable. "Be willing to listen to the critique and not take it personally," Baxter suggests.

With a little research a writer can find a conference that suits his or her needs and budget. Our advice to any writer is simple. Go to conferences. Get to know other writers and editors. The relationships you form there can pay big dividends in the years to come. Check out the ECPA Web site for links to conferences, writers services, and other information for writers—www.ecpa.org. Also go to Sally Stuart's site for conference and other valuable information—www.stuartmarket.com. Another excellent source is Christian Writers Fellowship International. Their magazine, *Cross & Quill,* has conference information and other data: www.cwfionline.org. Writers Information Network (WIN), headed by Elaine Wright Colvin, is an organization that has up-to-date information on conferences and many other items that writers will find valuable: www.christianwritersinfo.net.

Best Sellers and the Marketing Machine

One of the most interesting phenomena in recent religious publishing is wider cultural acceptance of books and other media by Christian writers. Books especially have seen a rise in sales during the past decade. Once these books were sold almost exclusively in Christian bookstores. Today, however, best sellers are found everywhere, including the large discount retailers like Wal-Mart and Target. That creates some interesting dynamics since those retailers typically sell books for up to 40 percent less than a full-price bookstore.

In an article by Rob Moll in *Christianity Today,* Bill Anderson, president and CEO of ICR, International Christian Retailers Association, sees the irony of the rising sales of books but the struggle of Christian bookstores. He says, "We've got a little bit of a catch-22 here. We used to complain that not enough people knew that Christian books existed. As more people have become aware, America's retailers want to sell them, and that has increased our competition." The result is that while *The Purpose Driven Life* can be purchased at Borders or on Amazon.com, many of the mom-and-pop Christian bookstores that used to handle this sort of book are going out of business. For example, between 2000 and 2002 the general Christian product market grew by $200 million, but Christian stores saw their business shrink by $100 million, according to Rob Moll. Hundreds of Christian retailers have closed their doors as their traditional customers went to the big-box stores.

What does this mean for writers? For one thing, we need to realize that the market for Christian books is shifting. The once-stable niche of the stand-alone bookstore is changing rapidly. Many customers will purchase their books at the big-box retailers although others will continue to support the local Christian bookstore. A manager over a group of such stores says, "Customers should be able to trust what they find on the shelves of a CBA store as orthodox Christianity."

Publishers try to develop and maintain what they call their "branded authors," that is, writers with broad name recognition, such as Max Lucado, John Maxwell, Joyce Meyers and the like. These writers can deliver books that will sell hundreds of thousands of copies if not more. All this means that beginners have a tougher time breaking in and rising toward the top. They must work harder and write better than ever before.

Fiction

Christian fiction was once the domain of sweet stories about home and romance. Love was always chaste; and violence, if present at all, was implied. Only a handful of writers toiled in this field of the publishing garden, and few could actually make a living at it. To most people, "Christian fiction" represented the worst sort of unrealistic, pious "mind candy." Has that situation changed today!

This genre today is one of the fastest growing segments of any branch of publishing. Many credit Frank Peretti's 1986 novel, *This Present Darkness,* with breaking the barrier for Christian fiction. Besides selling 2.5 million copies and making Peretti's career, it opened the doors to a kind of fiction that was more than innocuous love stories. Some say it introduced a healthy dose of realism into Christian fiction.

In 1990 about five hundred "faith fiction" titles were in print. By 2005 that number had risen five times. In 2004 alone four hundred new titles were added. *Publishers Weekly* reports, "What was once perceived as vanilla reads for ladies of a certain age now runs the gamut of genres, including mysteries, fantasy, science fiction—and even a growing body of more literary titles."

Today some writers are writing as Christians but do not want to be identified as a "Christian writer." Scott Derrickson is one such artist. He is a writer and director who is also a sought-after screenwriter. Derrickson explains that he has faith, but that does not mean that he tries to force his faith onto others. In an article in *NRB,* the magazine of National Religious Broadcasters, he says, "Jesus didn't tell explicitly 'Christian' stories. Many of his parables are about everyday life, and they impacted people in a powerful way. I want the movies I work on to do the same thing. When you tell a great story, people drop their defenses and give you the opportunity to share profound truth. But if they feel like you're preaching to them, they'll quickly resist and the opportunity is lost."

Apparently some other writers think that way too. One of the trends in Christian fiction publishing is the production of what some call "unsanitized" novels. Marcia Ford, in a *Publishers Weekly* article, quotes Dudley Delffs, an editor at WaterBrook, as saying, "Readers are tired of novels driven by a dogmatic evangelical agenda in which flat characters interact in a sanitized world. They discovered well-written general market novels that include realistic and compelling faith elements, so they would like to see the same in Christian bookstores." Ford also quotes Allen Arnold, publisher of WestBow, an imprint of Thomas Nelson, who says, "Our primary goal isn't 'edgy' fiction but stories with real, authentic voice that are entertaining, culturally relevant, and God honoring. When we find those voices, we don't shy away from the edgy elements—or sugarcoat them."

Is dealing with the reality of life anything new in publishing? Arnold simply points people back to the Bible. He says the Bible is filled with stories of the realities of evil. It never glorifies evil, though. Instead, it portrays it for what it is and the results that come from it. Likewise, Christian fiction reveals the ugliness of sin. "The darker it is, the more repulsive it is—and the more powerful God is." Arnold summarizes the thinking of many people in the Christian publishing industry today: "We don't exist in a Norman Rockwell painting or a Mr. Rogers's neighborhood or a Precious Moments village. Jesus doesn't save us from real life. We follow him through the nitty-gritty real world right where we are. When we create stories that don't shy away from reality, God's power is even more visible as the true light in our fallen world."

In a profile on novelist Bret Lott in *Christianity Today,* Lauren F. Winner notes that many writers are beginning to bring their talents for telling a compelling story to religious publishing. They write naturally from a Christian worldview but not overtly preachy or with heavy-handed methods. Lott, whose novel *Jewel* was selected by Oprah Winfrey for her book club, says that his writing is not a demand but an invitation. "I'm a Christian who's a writer. I'm not a Christian writer, so to speak." So what is the difference?

Lott explains it this way: "If people are going to read my books, they're not going to encounter the traditional salvation scene. C. S. Lewis once said that we don't need more books about Christians; we need more books with Christian values built into them. That's what I'm trying to do in my fiction. I'm not trying to write Christian fiction that preaches to the choir. The choir already knows the drill."

This brings up a point still being debated in Christian publishing circles. How should life—with all its ugliness and degradation—be portrayed? While some publishers seem to opt for clean, almost sanitized depictions of the human situation, others are beginning to open up to other possibilities. Bret Lott asks, "If we can't portray sin, then how will we know it when we see it?" He continues, "Christ hung with the sinners. He knew what sin was. If we act like the only thing that ought to be portrayed with the written word is the 'gee willikers' type of bad guy, then we're forgetting about the two robbers who died with Jesus. We're forgetting about the adulterous woman. We're forgetting about the tax collector."

Lott, and a whole host of other novelists, is working to produce "faith-infused" fiction. The process of redemption and the themes of grace and divine love are woven into the fabric of the story and not just dropped into it in a willy-nilly fashion. Jenny Baumgarten, an editor at WestBow, the fiction imprint of Thomas Nelson, speaks of this new quality of fiction. In Lauren Winner's article in *Christianity Today,* Baumgarten says, "Our whole vision is to partner with authors writing from a Christian worldview who are writing great fiction; Bret Lott is the poster boy for that. He's writing great fiction, and he's a Christian, and his worldview bleeds into his novels in a way that is not trite or formulaic."

Another trend in fiction, some would say the direct opposite of "realistic fiction," is what is being called "moral fiction." This is fiction that seeks to tell great stories about interesting people in everyday situations but in ways that are not in-your-face aggressive. In an Associated Baptist Press story, Ted Parks cites novelist Nicholas Sparks as a master of this sort of fiction. Sparks's books, and movies made from them, such as *The Notebook* and *Message in a Bottle,* have inspired millions of readers and viewers. Sparks does not use profanity in his novels. His characters' lives center on "faith, family, community, friendships." Sparks says his writing has a definite spiritual dimension to it. "When I'm writing well, I feel the presence of God. I feel this enormous sense of completion and wonder and awe at the gift that I've been given."

Dale Brown directs the annual Festival of Faith and Writing at Calvin College in Grand Rapids, Michigan. He sees that morally inoffensive fiction is finding a healthy place in publishing. He cites Jan Karon as an example of this sort of writer, one who "talks about trying to write about goodness rather than sin."

What is fiction, and how does it operate? At its simplest, fiction is life wrapped up in invented situations and characters.

What does it do? Fiction takes us into new worlds—sometimes literally as in science fiction. But even when it is earth-based, fiction gives us another pair of spectacles with which to view life. It transports us via imagination into another place and lets us walk around in another's shoes. The old proverb attributed to American Indians is true—to understand someone else, walk in his moccasins.

Your authors of this book, Don and Len, are white males. That gives a particular perspective to the way we experience life. But we can read powerful fiction that shows us what life is like for a black female, a Hispanic teenager, an Asian grandmother, an inner-city postal worker, a poverty-bound unwed mother, and a million other combinations of life styles and choices.

In short, fiction is life—life with all its varied complexities, moments of grace, and experiences of redemption. Open-eyed novelists with skill and imagination can open windows that readers can see through and glimpse other worlds unknown. In the hands of gifted writers like T. Davis Bunn, Jan Karon, and Jack Cavanaugh, the novel can be an RSVP by which God bids the reader to come to the party. It can be a fulcrum on which a seemingly ruined life can be levered to a higher level. The imaginary world of fiction can be the key to unlock those places in a reader's heart that she may not even be aware of, those places where God wants to inhabit and bring real life.

Christian novelists cannot afford to pander fluff while their secular counterparts are capturing hearts with the sheer force of their abilities to tell believable stories. That is why we should work hard to learn the craft and then use it to influence lives for Christ. In his book *On Writing: A Memoir of the Craft,* novelist Stephen King talks about the fact that John Grisham knows the law and lawyers and writes convincingly about them. King says, "What *you* know makes you unique in some other way. Be brave. Map the enemy's positions, come back, and tell us all you know."

In order to do that, King says we have to keep our minds open and ready to see what others might miss. This is how he explains the process of formulating an idea for a novel: "Let's get one thing clear right now, shall we? There is no Idea Dump, no Story Central, no Island of the Buried Bestsellers; good story ideas seem to come quite literally from nowhere, sailing at you right out of the empty sky: two previously unrelated ideas come together and make something new under the sun. Your job isn't to find these ideas but to recognize them when they show up."

In fiction the writer imagines a "what-if" situation and then fills it with people whom readers can identify with, at least at some level. In order to achieve that deep level of connection between the written word and the reader, the writer has to search deep inside the self to know what hurts and what heals, what stings and what blesses, what

the darkest corners of life are, and where the ligh
found. For too long so-called Christian fiction did not
really deal with life at its fullest. The situations seemed
contrived, and the characters seemed plastic and one
dimensional. Nick Harrison, senior editor at Harvest
House, spoke about this in the journal *The Win-Informer*:

> Wonderfully drawn characters are the
> benchmark of literary novels. But I see the same
> stereotypical heroine in many manuscripts. She
> could be lifted out of one book and set down in
> another, and most readers wouldn't notice the
> difference. I'm looking for original characters.
> Anne Tyler characters. The market is competitive.
> Aspiring Christian authors must be excellent to
> be published at the best Christian publishing
> houses today. They can't write like they did 10
> years ago and expect to find success. Some novels
> published in CBA only a few years ago might not
> be published if they were submitted today.

When Stephen King was in school, many writers, especially the poets, thought writing was just "catching" the
inspiration. He says, "There was a view among the student
writers I knew at that time that good writing came spon-
taneously, in an uprush of feeling that had to be caught at
once; when you were building that all-important stairway
to heaven, you couldn't just stand around with your ham-
mer in your hand." He continues, "Would-be poets were
living in a dewy Tolkien-tinged world, catching poems
out of the ether. It was pretty much unanimous: serious art
came from . . . *out there!* Writers were blessed steno-
graphers taking divine dictation."

Some Christian writers think of their work in a similar fashion—"taking divine dictation." We contend this is a seriously mistaken view of writing. Writing is difficult work that can be learned through hard effort and practice. "Overnight success" usually takes a decade. While we do not agree with Stephen King on many things, this one idea of his gets our nod of approval. He has two convictions about writing: "The first is that good writing consists of mastering the fundamentals (vocabulary, grammar, the elements of style). . . . The second is that while it is impossible to make a competent writer out of a bad writer, and while it is equally impossible to make a great writer out of a good one, it *is* possible, with lots of hard work, dedication, and timely help, to make a good writer out of a merely competent one." We agree. Our goal for this book has been that readers would learn what is necessary to become good writers and, having learned, would practice their craft with energy and imagination.

Today's publishing industry is a moving target. The bar for getting published is rising, and would-be authors must work harder to get their foot in the door and keep it open long enough to make a significant impact. That is possible, but it takes hard work and the willingness to face the challenges of getting published. If it were easy, everyone would be doing it!

Kurt Vonnegut imagined what the unformed world must look like from God's perspective. That image formed his advice for the writer: "A blank piece of paper is God's way of letting us know what it is like to be God."

You will sit at your desk staring at a blank piece of paper or an empty computer screen wondering what sort of world you might create. Sometimes the words flow easily. At other times you feel you are doing oral surgery, cutting them out of yourself one letter at a time. But a writer who has something to say will find a way, regardless of the obstacles. In his autobiography, *The Oak and the Calf,* Alexandr Solzhenitsyn recalls how he "wrote" in the concentration camps, where writing was forbidden, and how vulnerable his work was.

> In the camp, this meant committing my verse—many thousands of lines—to memory. To help me with this, I improvised decimal counting beads and, in transit to prisons, broke up matchsticks and used the fragments as tallies. As I approached the end of my sentence, I grew more confident of my powers of memory, and began writing down and memorizing prose—dialogue at first, but then, bit by bit, whole densely written passages. . . . But more and more of my time—in the end as much as one week every month—went into the regular repetition of all I had memorized.
>
> Then came exile, and right at the beginning of my exile, cancer. . . . In December [1953] the doctors—comrades in exile—confirmed that I had at most three weeks left. All that I had memorized in the camps ran the risk of extinction together with the head that held it. This was a dreadful moment in my life: to die on the threshold of freedom, to see all I had written, all that gave meaning to my life thus far, about to perish with me. . . .
>
> I hurriedly copied things out in tiny handwriting, rolled them, several pages at a time,

into tight cylinders and squeezed these into a champagne bottle. I buried the bottle in my garden—and set off for Tashkent to meet the new year and to die.

Solzhenitsyn was treated for his cancer and recovered completely. His work would later earn him the Nobel Prize, but he did not know any of that when he hoarded his words in the prison camp in Siberia. He just knew that he had to find a way to write. Whatever your challenges, you can find a way too. And when you do, your words will be worth reading because they were worth writing. Ecclesiastes 11:1 says, "Cast your bread upon the waters, for after many days you will find it again" (NIV). This is a commercial image of a merchant sending his goods across the sea in hopes of selling them at a profit. But the advice is good in any venture. Take the chance. Try. Do it with all your might. Give it your best shot. The worst that could happen is that you end up with soggy bread! On the other hand, you will never know what the return ship might be bringing back.

No, publishing is not for cowards. But it is for Christians. Enjoy the journey.

CHAPTER 11
A Sample Style Guide for Authors and Editors

Excerpted from *The Little Style Guide to Great Christian Writing and Publishing* by Leonard G. Goss and Carolyn Stanford Goss (Nashville, Tenn.: Broadman & Holman Publishers, 2004).

Book Production

A. Preparation of the Manuscript (2.3–.46)

1. It is the author's responsibility to provide copy (disk and printout) that is clear, readable, and accurate. The manuscript must be typed and double-spaced. It should have wide margins (1 inch) on good quality standard white bond paper 8 1/2 x 11 inches. Computer printouts should preferably be printed by a laser printer. Colored paper or flimsy onionskin is not acceptable, for it is soon reduced to tatters in the editorial office. Print only one side of the paper.

2. The manuscript must be complete. Additions and corrections are confusing and difficult to add once the

manuscript has been accepted for publication. The author should include the following parts with the book:

> Title Page
> Table of Contents
> All text matter
> Footnotes on separate pages, at end of book,
>   not in a running footnotes window
> Tables or graphs on separate pages
> Bibliography
> Indexes (prepared by author after final proofs
>   are available)

3. The manuscript pages should be numbered consecutively in the upper *right* corner. Do *not* number them by chapter (3–1, 3–2, etc.). Sheets inserted after the manuscript has been paginated should carry the preceding page number with *a, b, c* added: *86a, 86b, 86c.* If a page is later removed, the preceding page should be double numbered: 106–7.

4. It is the author's responsibility to check all Scripture references, quotations, and footnotes for accuracy prior to submitting the manuscript.

5. All books must be sent on either disk or CD, in Microsoft Word or a program compatible with it. The disk must be Macintosh or IBM compatible.

B. Rights and Permissions (4.11–.98)

1. The publisher will prepare the copyright page and also has the privilege to give permission to reprint excerpts in other publications.

2. If the author wishes to use a portion of a copyrighted work and there is some question whether the kind or

amount of the material exceeds a fair use, the author should request permission to quote the portion in question. It is the author's responsibility to obtain permission to quote from other sources. Notice of the original copyright and permission to reprint must appear either on the copyright page of the book or in a footnote on the first page of the reprinted material or in a special list of acknowledgments. All permissions or copies of them must be sent to the publisher.

3. The author is further responsible for any fees charged by grantors of permission unless the author makes other arrangements with the grantor. When the publisher pays the cost of procuring permission rights, the publisher generally deducts these costs from the author's future royalties.

4. Frequent use of modern Scripture versions may require permission.

C. Stages in Manuscript Production (2.50, 3.43)

1. An edited manuscript usually passes through the following stages in the production process:

> Sample page and design
> Typesetting
> First proofs (copy sent to author)
> Second and additional proofs (if necessary)
> Final proofs
> Camera copy
> Platemaking
> Press
> Binding

2. Once page proofs (final proofs) are made, revisions are costly and should be minimal. Major changes at this stage in production are not acceptable. Corrections should be confined to substantive errors.

3. Authors will receive final proofs *only* if the book requires an index. In this case, the author will receive a deadline to complete the index, but manuscript revisions are not made at this time.

D. The Editor-Author Relationship

1. During the editorial process, editors work with authors to produce books that are as excellent as they can be, in terms of both content and quality. Editing is usually done on screen—sometimes only for house style, sometimes in a more comprehensive way, depending on the specific needs of a given manuscript.

2. As editors edit an assigned book, they typically correct misspellings, punctuation errors, and incorrect word usage, and generally conform the book to house style. The editor also identifies and, in cooperation with the author, clarifies unclear writing, theological or historical inaccuracies, and potentially offensive material.

3. Some see the editor as a supercritical, academic-monastic individual who cackles as he edits a manuscript so heavily that writers can't recognize their own work. Others idealize the editor as a knight in shining armor who will rescue a manuscript (or an author) from obscurity, make the work great, and bring huge success! The truth is somewhere in between.

In Christian publishing, the editor and the writer have the same goals and serve the same Lord, but they are coming to the task from different angles. This sometimes makes for a nebulous world in which the rules seem unclear. Ideally, author and editor will maintain a context of cooperation and teamwork, and within that context the editor fills necessary roles on behalf of both the publisher and the author. The editor and the writer are coworkers.

Throughout the editorial process the editor gives honest feedback and offers constructive criticism. If some elements in the book do not work, are offensive to the intended readership, are theologically questionable or simply unclear, it is the editor's responsibility to work with the author to resolve the problem.

Trust is at the core of the editor-author relationship. The editor respects the writer's point of view, the purpose for the book, the style, and so on, and thus doesn't make the book the editor's rather than the writer's. On the other hand, the writer trusts the editor to tell him what the book is really like and what its strengths and weaknesses are. The editor helps a writer focus on a reading audience, on the purpose for writing the book, and on whether the story line, tone, writing flow and style, content, and vocabulary effectively reach intended readers. The editor helps the author remember that quality is just as important as content.

Punctuation

A. Period (6.13–.17)

1. Use a period without parentheses after numerals or letters in a vertical listing.

1. a.
2. b.
3. c.

2. Enclose numerals or letters in a list within a paragraph in double parentheses, or use an end parenthesis after a numeral or letter. Do not follow them with a period in either case.

> Some of the earliest texts of the New Testament have been found in (1) Oxyrhynchus Papyrus 657, (2) Chester Beatty Papyrus II, and (3) Bodmer Papyrus II.

3. Omit the period after running heads, centered headlines, and signatures.

4. Place periods within quotation marks.

> Professor Joseph's favorite saying was "There is no such thing as a dumb question."

> The would-be theologian took up residence in a cave, thinking he would thus avoid succumbing to 'the social gospel.'

B. Exclamation Point (6.76–.79)

1. Use the exclamation point to mark an emphatic or sarcastic comment.

> How beautiful is the girl in my arms!

> He seems to enjoy being miserable!

2. Place the exclamation within quotation marks, parentheses, or brackets when it is part of the quoted or parenthetical material; otherwise, place it outside the quotation marks.

> "Don't hang me," cried the captured rustler, "I'm innocent!"

> The traitor betrayed everyone, including his "friends"!

C. Question Mark (6.70–.75)

1. The question mark is used to pose a question or to express an editorial doubt.

> What is the sound of one hand clapping?
>
> *How will this affect my future?* he was thinking.
>
> The translation of the Bible made by Miles Coverdale (1488?–1569) was used to a great extent by the translators of the 1611 Authorized Version.

2. Questions within a sentence that consist of single words, such as *who, when, how,* or *why* do not require a question mark. It is better to italicize the word.

> The question is not *how* but *when.*

3. Place the question mark inside quotation marks, parentheses, or brackets when it is part of the quoted or parenthetical material.

> "Barry, did you tell your music director that you love to sing?"

4. Place the question mark outside the quotation marks when the quoted material is not a question.

> When you finish work, will you hear Jesus say, "Well done"?

5. When a question is a rhetorical one that is not meant to elicit information but is made as a more striking substitute for a statement, it does not always require a question mark. Depending on the context, it can end with a period, a comma, or even an exclamation point.

> "Who in the world would send a vampire novel to B&H!" Kim was obviously exasperated.

6. Indirect questions do not require a question mark.

> Gary asked if he could go to the writing conference.

D. Comma (6.18–.56)

A comma is used to indicate the smallest pause in continuity of thought or sentence structure. The modern practice is to pause infrequently, especially if the meaning is clear without an interruption. Aside from a few set rules, its use is a matter of good judgment.

1. Use a comma before the conjunction uniting two parts of a compound sentence unless both parts are very short.

> Carol's biscotti are pretty good, but her zwieback is the best in the county.

> Trent drove to Borders and he walked to Corky's Barbecue.

2. Use commas to set off an adjectival phrase or clause that is nonrestrictive and could be dropped without changing the reference of the noun.

> The apostle Paul, a peace-loving man, was often the target of violence from nonbelievers during his ministry.

3. Use commas to set off interjecting transitional adverbs and similar elements that effect a distinct break in the continuity of thought.

> All people of goodwill, therefore, must remain vigilant.

4. In most cases, it is best to set off a word, phrase, or clause in apposition to a noun.

> One of his brothers, Edward, is a senior partner in a well-respected law firm.

If, however, the appositive has a restrictive function, do not set it off by a comma.

> His son David is a starving actor.

5. Set off two or more adjectives by commas if each one modifies the noun alone.

> Timothy proved himself to be an honest, hardworking servant.

Exception: If the first adjective modifies the idea expressed by the combination of the second adjective and the noun, no comma is needed.

> The hungry old tiger licked his chops when he saw the missionary stumble into the clearing.

[One method to determine this usage is to ask if the word *and* can be inserted between the two modifiers without changing the meaning of the sentence or making it awkward. If it cannot, no comma is required.]

6. In a series of three or more elements, place a comma before the conjunction.

> According to legend, Vladimir studied Islam, Judaism, and Roman Catholicism before deciding to become a Christian.

7. Use commas to set off words identifying a title or position after a name.

> Nero, the cruel and bloodthirsty emperor who murdered Christians, was also responsible for the burning of Rome.

8. Use commas to indicate the date and to set off names of geographical places.

> May 30, 1949 (Alternate style: 30 May 1949)
>
> He was born on December 31, 1947, in San Diego, California, and later moved to Arizona.

9. Usually it is preferable to set off a dependent clause that precedes the main clause by a comma.

> If you go to the store, please get some bananas.

10. In most cases, separate a direct quotation or maxim from the rest of the sentence by commas.

> "I am sorry," said the lawyer sadly, "that I can be of no help."

If the quote is restrictive appositive or used as the subject or predicate nominative, it should not be set off with commas.

> "When pigs fly" was a phrase Len least expected.

E. Semicolon (6.57–.62)

A semicolon marks a more important break in sentence flow than one marked by a comma.

1. Use a semicolon between two independent clauses not connected by a conjunction.

> Novels are steady moneymakers; particularly good sellers are apocalyptic stories.

2. The following adverbs should be preceded by a semicolon when used between clauses for a compound sentence: *then, however, thus, hence, indeed, accordingly, besides,* and *therefore.* The exception to this rule involves clauses introduced by the adverbs *yet* and *so,* which are preceded by a comma.

> Lindsay forgot about volleyball practice; therefore, she did not play in the game.
>
> Joseph has made plans to finish graduate school, yet his course work is not complete.

3. Use a semicolon as an alternate way to separate a long compound sentence when either part of the sentence has a comma break.

> Silvia is an even-tempered, happy person, who always greets others with a smile; and she has a deep faith in God, remaining calm when difficulties arise.

4. You may choose to use semicolons for emphasis.

> It was the best of times; it was the worst of times.

5. Use semicolons to separate references (particularly Bible references) when they contain internal punctuation.

> Luke 1:1–4; 2:14, 21; 5:12, 14, 16.

6. Use semicolons for clarity to separate items in a long or complex series.

> The total number of those attending the conference was editors, 65; publishers, 30; writers, 47.

7. Always place semicolons outside quotation marks and parentheses.

> Luther once called the book of James "the epistle of straw"; however, he wrote a brilliant commentary on it.

F. Colon (6.63–.69)

A colon marks a discontinuity of grammatical construction greater than that indicated by a semicolon but less than a period. Its main function is to introduce material that follows immediately.

1. You may use a colon to emphasize a sequence in thought between two clauses that form a single sentence.

> Many in the congregation helped with the bake sale: twenty of them, for example, made pies.

2. A colon can also introduce a list or series.

> Nashville has at least three important tourist attractions: Broadway, Music Row, and LifeWay.

(If, however, the series is introduced by *namely, for instance, for example,* or *that is,* do not use a colon unless the series consists of one or more grammatically complete clauses: Nashville has at least three important tourist attractions, namely, Broadway, Music Row, and LifeWay.)

3. Use a colon between chapter and verse in Scripture passages.

> Matt. 2:5–13

G. Dash (6.80–.96)

1. Use an en dash to indicate inclusive or continuing numbers, as in dates, page references or Scripture references.

> pp. 23–46
>
> 1861–65
>
> January–May 1994
>
> Acts 2:35–5:14

2. Use an em dash (—) to denote an abrupt break in thought that affects sentence structure.

> The emperor—he had been awake half the night waiting in vain for a reply—came down to breakfast in an angry mood.

3. Use a 2-em dash (no space on either side) to indicate missing letters in a word.

> Melody P——k voted no.

4. Use a 3-em dash (with space on each side) to indicate that a whole word has been omitted.

> The ship left ——— in May.

H. Quotation Marks (6.8–10, 11.1–.50)

1. Direct quotations must reproduce exactly the wording, spelling, and punctuation of the original, with one exception: It is acceptable to change the initial letter of the quotation to a capital or lowercase letter to fit the syntax of the text. Typographical errors that appear in

modern works may be corrected, but idiosyncrasies of spelling in older works should be observed.

2. It is the author's responsibility to check every quotation against the original for accuracy.

3. Set quotations over eight lines in block quotes. You may insert shorter quotations within the text.

4. If the quotation, either run into or set off from the text, is used as part of the author's sentence, it begins with a lowercase letter, even though the original is a complete sentence and begins with a capital letter.

> The gospel of John begins with the assertion that "in the beginning was the Word."

5. Direct conversation, whether run into or set off from the text, should always be enclosed in quotation marks.

> Travis protested, "I simply do not like the taste of tofu in food!" He had just finished eating a small bowl of tofu chili. "Ugh! Tofu has no taste, in my opinion."
>
> "That's precisely why some people like it," Katie explained.

6. Quoted material set off from the text as a block quotation should not be enclosed in quotation marks. Quoted material within a block quotation should be enclosed in double quotation marks, even if the source used single quotation marks.

7. Scripture used in block quotations must be followed by the reference in parentheses. Another method is to put the reference on a separate line, with an em dash before and no parentheses.

8. The words *yes* and *no* should not be quoted except in direct discourse.

> Joshua always answered yes; he could not say no.

I. Parentheses (6.97–.103)

1. You may use parentheses, like commas and dashes, to set off amplifying, explanatory, or digressive elements. Use commas, however, if the two parts are closely related.

> He had long suspected that the inert gasses (helium, neon, argon, krypton) could be used to produce a similar effect.

2. You may enclose expressions such as *that is, namely, e.g., i.e.,* and the element introduced in parentheses if the break in thought is greater than that signaled by a comma.

> Bones from several animals (e.g., a dog, a cat, a squirrel, a pigeon) were found in the grave.

3. Use parentheses to enclose numerals or letters marking divisions or enumerations run into the text.

> The anthropologist stated there were no inexplicable differences between (1) Java man, (2) Neanderthal man, and, (3) Cro-Magnon man.

4. Place ending punctuation outside a closing parenthesis if the word or phrase in the parentheses interrupts or is interjected into a sentence. When a question mark or an exclamation point is part of the parenthetical matter, place the question mark or exclamation point inside the closing parenthesis.

> A consistent format should be followed (do not punctuate by ear).

> A consistent format should be followed (never punctuate by ear!).

5. You can follow ending punctuation of a sentence by separate parenthetical matter that is also a sentence or

complete thought. The parenthetical matter may be related to but independent of the previous sentence.

> Was this a desperate cry for help? (Or any one of a hundred other considerations?)

6. When quoting Scripture, place the period after the parentheses containing the reference. If the quotation requires a question mark or exclamation point, place it with the text, and place the period after the last parenthesis. When quoting Scripture that is set off from the text as a block quotation, place the period after the Scripture text.

> "In the beginning God created the heaven and the earth" (Gen. 1:1).

> "Lord, are You going to wash my feet?" (John 13:6).

J. Brackets (6.104–.110)

1. Brackets enclose editorial interpolations, corrections, explanations, or comments.

> Jesus told Nicodemus, "Unless someone is born again [born anew, or born from above] he cannot see the Kingdom of God."

> He [Robert E. Lee] died in 1870, never having received a pardon from the United States government.

2. Brackets may also enclose the phonetic transcript of a word.

> He attributed the light to the phenomenon called *gegenschein* [ga-gen-shin].

K. Ellipses (11.51–.71)

1. Indicate any omission of a word, phrase, line, or paragraph from a quoted passage by ellipsis points, with a space before and after each dot.

2. Three dots . . . indicate that material is deleted at the beginning or within a sentence.

> "By faith Moses . . . was hidden by his parents . . .
> because they saw that the child was beautiful"
> (Heb. 11:23).

3. You may use other punctuation on either side of the three ellipsis dots if it makes the meaning clearer.

> I wondered, was he the hapless dupe he made out to
> be? . . . He seemed far too clever for that.

4. Three dots . . . may also indicate a break in thought, daydreaming, or hesitation. Use an en dash, however, to indicate an *external* interruption of speech or thought.

> If he had only come sooner . . . if only . . . then perhaps
> everything would have been different. I—that is, we—
> yes, we wish he had come sooner.

5. Unless the content requires such, it is not usually necessary to use ellipsis points before or after a verse or a portion of a Scripture verse. Introductory words such as *and* and *for* may be omitted from a Scripture quotation without using ellipsis points.

> "For God loved the world in this way . . ." (John 3:16)
> may correctly read "God loved the world in this
> way . . ."

6. Four dots . . . . indicate that material is omitted at the end of a sentence (the extra dot accounts for the period). The missing material could be (1) the last part of a quoted sentence, (2) the first part of the next sentence, (3) a whole sentence or more, or (4) a whole paragraph or more.

> "Now all the believers were together and had every-
> thing in common. . . . Every day they devoted them-
> selves to meeting together" (Acts 2:44, 46).

7. If the original quotation is punctuated with a question mark or an exclamation point, retain this mark and use three dots for the ellipsis.

> "Now is my soul troubled. What should I say—'Father, save me from this hour?' . . . Father, glorify your name!" (John 12:27).

L. Apostrophe (7.17–.32)

1. The apostrophe is the mark of the possessive. The possessive case of singular nouns is formed by the addition of an apostrophe and an s, and the possessive of plural nouns by the addition of an apostrophe only.

> the book's cover
> the puppies' tails

2. When you can do it without confusion, form the plural of numbers and letters used as words by adding s alone.

> the three Rs
> four YMCAs
> the early 1930s

3. Abbreviations with periods, lowercase letters used as nouns, and some capital letters may require an apostrophe for clarity, even when not used in a possessive sense.

> M.Div.'s   x's and y's
> Th.D.'s   S's, A's, I's

4. The general rule for forming the possessive of common nouns (apostrophe and an s for singular names, an s followed by an apostrophe for plural names—see number 1 above) also applies to proper names, including most names of any length ending in sibilants.

Susie's swimming pool

Steve's messy office

Rosses' house (but Ross's house, when the word refers to just one person)

Burns's poems

Exceptions: The names Jesus and Moses are traditional exceptions to the general rule for forming the possessive.

Jesus' disciples

Moses' staff

M. Solidus/Slash/Slant/Virgule (6.111–.119)

1. Related to the dash and the hyphen in form and function, the solidus (/) sometimes indicates alternatives and alternative word forms or spellings and replaces *and* in some sentences.

Qur'an/Koran

Sales figures rose dramatically in the June/July period.

Miss Holley's bridal bouquet will feature daisies and/or primroses.

2. A solidus with no spaces before or after can indicate that a time period spans two consecutive years, though the en dash is preferable.

Winter 1910/11 or Winter 1910–11 (preferable)

3. When poetry or text from songs is run into the text, a solidus with a space both before and after it designates line breaks.

As Thomas Gray once observed, "Full many a flower was born to blush unseen / And waste its sweetness on the desert air."

N. Diacritical Marks and Special Characters (10.14)

English is one of very few languages that can be set without accents, diacritics, or special alphabetic characters for native words. Editors and typesetters may recognize the more common marks used in foreign words such as *¿, á, è,* or *ñ,* but may not be familiar with ones used in other languages (i.e., classical Greek, Hebrew, or Chinese). Authors need to mark their manuscripts clearly when they use such a mark or notify the editor if there will be a need to use a special typeface.

Elements of Style

A. Italics (7.49–.81)

1. The use of italics can emphasize a word or phrase.

> But the *actual* cause of the accident is yet to be determined.

2. It is often helpful to set a technical term, especially when it is accompanied by its definition, in italics the first time it appears in the text.

> *Tabular matter* is copy, usually consisting of figures, which is set in columns.

3. Italicize isolated words or phrases in a foreign language if they are unfamiliar to most readers.

> *Caveat Emptor!*
> *Ein feste Burg ist unser Gott*
> *sine qua non*

Exception: You do not need to italicize foreign expressions used so commonly that they have become a recognized part of the English language.

| per se | ad hoc | quid pro quo | Wiener schnitzel |
| ad lib | hacienda | habeas corpus | coup de grace |

4. To clarify a person's thoughts in contrast to one's verbal discourse, italics is a good choice.

> I looked over the unarmed bushwhacker who was attempting to rob me. *He can't be serious,* I thought to myself.

5. Italicize references to words as words.

> The word *faith* has often been confused with hope.

6. Use italics for book titles, movies, ships, and for radio or TV programs in continuing series. Set titles of individual programs not in continuing series in Roman type and quotation marks.

> *Screwtape Letters*
>
> USS *Yorktown*
>
> *Gunsmoke*
>
> NBC's series, *West Wing*
>
> "Beverly Sills Sings at the Met"

B. Hyphenation (7.81–.90)

1. Use hyphens cautiously. Most compound words do not require a hyphen. Most noun combinations that were formerly hyphenated are now written as solid words: butterfat, willpower. Others are still hyphenated: well-being. Some that were once hyphenated are now two words: water supply. Keep a copy of *Merriam-Webster's*

Collegiate Dictionary, Eleventh Edition on hand so as not to hyphenate by intuition.

2. A word or phrase used as an adjective is often hyphenated, but it may not be hyphenated when used as a noun.

> soul-winning program
>
> Soul winning (noun) was her mission.

3. Dividing a word for typographical purposes is tricky. If not sure where to divide, consult the *Merriam Webster's Collegiate Dictionary, Eleventh Edition,* and/or *Chicago Manual of Style, Fifteenth Edition,* Sections 7.33–.45.

C. Abbreviations (15.1–.76)

1. Do not use abbreviations for given names (unless the person himself wrote his name in that fashion).

> William not Wm.
>
> Charles not Chas.

2. When you use a civil or military title with the surname alone, spell out the individual's title.

> General Eisenhower
>
> Lieutenant Jenkins

If you use the person's full name and title, however, you may abbreviate the title.

> Sen. Bill Frist
>
> Col. Jack Papworth Goss

3. Always use the standard abbreviations for Mr., Mrs., Ms., and Dr.

4. Add the article *the* to the title *Reverend.* When you abbreviate the title, you may drop the article, but it should be accompanied by a full name (except in fiction).

the Reverend Billy Sunday
the Reverend Mr. Sunday
Rev. Billy Sunday

5. It is proper style to abbreviate the names of government agencies, organizations, associations, some corporations, and other groups. In most cases, set these abbreviations in capitals without periods.

NATO	ASPCA	ABC Network
ECPA	CBA	WPLN, Nashville Public Radio
AAR/SBL	SBC	NAPCE

The same applies to famous persons known by their initials only.

FDR	RFK

6. Always spell out the names of states, territories, and possessions of the United States when they stand alone in text.

The state of Arizona

Charlie moved to Nashville, Tennessee, to try his luck in the country music business.

7. Spell out the names of countries in the text. (*United States* is preferred over *U.S.* (United States used as an adjective may be abbreviated to U.S. in informal writing, i.e., U.S. currency.)

8. Spell out names of the months in the text, whether alone or in dates. It is acceptable form to abbreviate them in chronologies or footnotes.

Jan.	July
Feb.	Aug.
Mar.	Sept.
Apr.	Oct.

May	Nov.
June	Dec.

9. Always spell out the names of the days of the week.

10. It is standard style to abbreviate parts of a book in footnotes or bibliographies, but do not abbreviate them in the text.

appendix	app.
book	bk.
figure	fig.
folio	fol.
notes(s)	n. (plural is nn.)
number	no.
page(s)	p. (plural is pp.)
paragraph	par.
volume	vol. (plural is vols.)

D. Abbreviations and Scripture References (15.47–.54)

1. In text, spell out references to whole books or whole chapters of the Bible.

> The opening chapters of Ephesians . . .

> Genesis records the creation of the world in the first two chapters.

2. You may abbreviate biblical references when you enclose them in parentheses. In some scholarly or reference works and under some conditions, you may abbreviate them in the text.

Old Testament

Gen.	2 Chron.	Dan.
Exod.	Ezra	Hosea
Lev.	Neh.	Joel

Num.	Esther	Amos
Deut.	Job	Obad.
Josh.	Ps.	Jonah
Judg.	Prov.	Mic.
Ruth	Eccles.	Nah.
1 Sam.	Song of Sol.	Hab.
2 Sam.	Isa.	Zeph.
1 Kings	Jer.	Hag.
2 Kings	Lam.	Zech.
1 Chron.	Ezek.	Mal.

New Testament

Matt.	Eph.	Heb.
Mark	Phil.	James
Luke	Col.	1 Pet.
John	1 Thess.	2 Pet.
Acts	2 Thess.	1 John
Rom.	1 Tim.	2 John
1 Cor.	2 Tim.	3 John
2 Cor.	Titus	Jude
Gal.	Philem.	Rev.

Refer to books of the Bible with the title used in the version you cite. For example, the full name for Song of Solomon is "Song of Songs" in the *New International Version* and is not abbreviated.

3. Use Arabic numerals for all references. If the reference begins a sentence, however, spell out the number.

. . . in 1 John . . .

First John 3:16 says . . .

E. Abbreviations of Scripture Versions

It is standard practice to abbreviate versions of Scripture in references.

Amplified	*The Amplified Bible*
ASV	*American Standard Version*
AV	*Authorized (King James) Version*
CEV	*Contemporary English Version*
ESV	*English Standard Version*
GW	*God's Word: Today's Bible Translation*
JB	*Jerusalem Bible*
HCSB	*Holman Christian Standard Bible*
KJV	*King James Version* (also known as *Authorized Version*)
Lamsa	*The Holy Bible from Ancient Eastern Manuscripts*
LB	*Living Bible*
MLB	*Modern Language Bible/New Berkeley*
Moffatt	*A New Translation of the Bible*
NASB	*New American Standard Bible*
NASBU	*New American Standard Bible Update*
NCV	*New Century Version*
NEB	*New English Bible*
NET	*New Evangelical Translation*
NIV	*New International Version*
NJB	*New Jerusalem Bible*
NKJV	*New King James Version*
NLT	*New Living Translation*
NRSV	*New Revised Standard Version*
Phillips	*The New Testament in Modern English*
RNASB	*Revised New American Standard Bible*
RSV	*Revised Standard Version*
RV	*Revised Version*
SEB	*The Simple English Bible*
TEV	*Today's English Version*
TNIV	*Today's New International Version*

5. The abbreviation for verse is v. and for verses, vv.

   v. 23

   vv. 24–26

Use of Numbers in Text

A. General Rules (9.1–.71)

1. Write exact numbers under 100 as words and numbers 100 or larger in numerals.

> Our ten editors work tirelessly twenty-four hours a day.
>
> Joseph has at least 525 vintage baseball cards.
>
> The junior choir consisted of sixty children.

2. Spell out round numbers in hundreds, thousands, or millions, but list exact numbers larger than one hundred in numerals.

> four billion
>
> 3.6 billion
>
> 2,486
>
> 237

3. Two exceptions to this rule are year numbers and numbers referring to parts of the book.

> 44 BC   chapter 7
>
> AD 1999   page 7

4. Spell out initial numbers at the beginning of a sentence.

> One hundred forty years ago . . .
>
> Twenty-five percent . . .

5. Use commas between every group of three digits in figures of one thousand or more.

> 56,925
>
> 2,414

Exceptions to this rule are page numbers, addresses, and year numbers of four digits, which are written in figures without commas.

> He found the definition for *truffle* on page 1268.

6. In statistical, technical, or scientific copy, it is acceptable to write numbers that precede units of measurement as numerals, as well as to abbreviate the units. You may also use the ° symbol (the typographical symbol for *degrees*) for temperature measurement.

> 3 cubic inches
>
> 76 pounds
>
> 11 lb.
>
> 22 ft.
>
> 6 gal.
>
> 60 volts
>
> 32° F.
>
> 9 hrs.

7. In scientific and technical copy, use the symbol "%" for a percentage; in other copy, use the word *percent*.

> Of the citizens polled, more than 82% are in favor of the referendum.
>
> The loan has an interest rate of 7 percent.

In statistical or technical discussions, use numerals for percentages.

> The author claims that only 10 percent of evangelicals define themselves as doctrinal people.

8. Spell out percentages when they begin a sentence and when you use them in a literary or informal way.

> Ninety-nine percent of all editors think they are woefully underpaid.

> I imagine that ninety-seven percent of editors are book-
> worms.

9. Set decimal fractions, including academic grades, in figures, both in literary and scientific copy.

> A grade point average of 3.9 is considered outstanding.

10. Numbers applicable to the same category should be consistent throughout a paragraph. If the largest number contains three or more digits, use figures for all.

11. Where you use two adjacent numbers, spell out one of them for the sake of clarity.

> sixty 12-inch rulers
>
> 200 ten-cent stamps

12. Use a period without parentheses after numbers in a vertical listing.

> 1.
>
> 2.
>
> 3.

13. Enclose numerals in a list within a paragraph in double parentheses, or use an end parenthesis after a numeral. Do not follow the numeral with a period in either case.

> There were three areas of concern for the new
> product division: (1) production, (2) marketing, and
> (3) distribution.
>
> There were three areas of concern for the new product
> division: 1) production, 2) . . .

B. Currency (9.23–.29)

1. Follow general rules for numbers in regard to iso-lated references to money in United States currency, and

either spell them or represent them in figures as the rules specify.

> I'll give five dollars for the fund.

> Each employee received $42.20 for wages, $11.44 for benefits, and $2.40 for cost of living.

2. Substitute the words *million* and *billion* for zeros, but spell out round numbers in thousands.

> $6 million   ten thousand dollars

C. Dates and Times (9.33-.45)

1. Spell out in lowercase letters your references to particular centuries and decades.

> nineteenth century

> sixties and seventies (Exception: 1940s)

2. Write dates consistently in one of the following forms. Never use *st, nd, rd,* or *th* after figures in dates.

> October 14, 1964

> *Saturday Review,* 12 October 1968, 32

> The third of June 1943

> June 9 (never June 9th)

3. You should usually spell out times of day in the text.

> The church meeting wasn't over until four-thirty.

However, you may use figures to emphasize the exact time.

> The train arrived at 3:22.

4. Use numeric figures and regular capital letters in designations of time with AM or PM. Lowercase with periods is also accepable.

> 2:00 PM   8:25 a.m.

D. Street Names and Addresses (9.55–.57)

In most cases, represent house or highway numbers or street addresses in figures.

6556 North Glenwood

121 Beale Street

Interstate 57

Exceptions: Fifth Avenue, Forty-second Street, One LifeWay Plaza

Capitalization (8.1–.210)

A. Titles of Offices (8.21–.35)

1. Capitalize civil, military, religious, and professional titles when they immediately precede a personal name.

President McKinley

General Patton

Reverend C. A. Pagel

Chief Engineer Barry Dean

Cardinal Newman

2. In text matter, titles following a personal name or used alone in place of a name should be lowercase, with rare exceptions.

Abraham Lincoln, president of the United States

President Lincoln, the president of the United States

the president; presidential; presidency

General Ulysses S. Grant, commander in chief of the Union army

General Grant

the commander in chief
the general
George VI, king of England
the king of England; the king
the bishop of London
Edward J. Goss, counsel for the defense
Kari Drost, M.D.

3. Capitalize titles that you use in place of names in direct address.

I'm sorry, Officer, the accelerator stuck.

B. Kinship Names (8.39)

Put a kinship name in lowercase when it is not followed by a given name, but capitalize it in direct address or when you substitute the term for a personal name.

his father
my brothers and sister
Uncle Phil
Aunt Sara
Rosenberg is my mother's maiden name.
Ask Sister to give you a bite of hers.
Don't go near the water, Son.
Did you sell your house yet, Auntie?
Cheryl and Cindy are his youngest aunts.

C. Political Divisions (8.55–.56)

In general, capitalize words designating political divisions of the world, a country, state, city, and similar entities when they follow the name or when they are an accepted or official part of the name.

Roman Empire; but the empire under Diocletian; the empire

Washington State; the state of Washington

D. Organizations (8.66–.76)

1. Capitalize names of national and international organizations, movements and alliances, and members of political parties, but do not capitalize the words *movement, platform,* and similar terms.

Republican Party; Republican platform; Republicans(s)

Common Market

Loyalist(s)

Now is the time for all good men and women to come to the aid of their party.

2. Represent nouns and adjectives designating political and economic systems of thought and their proponents in lowercase, unless the term is used in a restricted, official way.

bolshevism

communism

democracy

democrat (a general advocate of democracy); democratic principles

republican (a general advocate of republicanism)

Marxism

E. Words Derived from Geographical Locations or Proper Names (8.46–.54, 8.64–.65)

Put words that have their root in geographical locations or proper names into lowercase when you choose them for their specialized meaning. (There are some exceptions, such as *Spanish moss;* if in doubt, check *Merriam Webster's Collegiate Dictionary, Eleventh Edition* or *Chicago Manual of Style, Fifteenth Edition.*)

dutch oven   india ink

french fries   diesel fuel

F. Holidays/Seasons (8.94–.96)

1. Lowercase the four seasons unless you personify them.

We welcomed the arrival of spring.

Then Winter—with her icy blasts—subsided.

2. Capitalize the names of religious holidays and seasons.

Christmas Eve

Easter, or Easter Sunday

Pentecost

Passover

3. Capitalize secular holidays and other specially designated days.

Fourth of July; the Fourth

Mother's Day

Thanksgiving Day

G. Religious Terms (8.97–.119)

1. Capitalize the names of the one supreme God.

God

Abba

Adonai

(the) Father

Logos

Jehovah

(the) Word

(the) Redeemer

Yahweh

(the) Savior

Master

(the) Son

Holy Spirit

Christ

2. Some Christian publishers differ from *The Chicago Manual of Style* in that they often capitalize pronouns referring to God in their books for the general reading audience. Check with your publisher regarding their preference and make consistent use of their rules. (Exceptions: Do not capitalize *who* or *whom*.)

Trust in Him.

God gives man what He wants.

Jesus and His disciples

Jesus knew He was the one who must die on the cross.

3. Though the names of specific places in Scripture are normally capitalized, put *heaven, hell,* and *hades* in lowercase.

4. Capitalize adjectives derived from proper names—e.g., Mosaic dispensation; Christian era; Maccabean period; Messianic age.

5. The following list of biblical and religious terms are capitalized or lowercased according to preferred style at most Christian publishers:

Abba
abomination of desolation, the
Abraham's Bosom
Abrahamic covenant
absolution
abyss, the
AD (AD 70 but 400 BC)
Adonai
adoptionism
Advent
Adventist(s)
adversary, the (Satan)
Advocate (Christ)
agape (Greek word for *love*)
agnosticism
Agnus Dei (Latin for *Lamb of God*)
AH (Anno Hebraica, in the Hebrew Year)
Albigensians
All Saints' Day (or All Hallows Eve)
All Souls' Day
Allah
alleluia
Almighty God
Almighty, the
Alpha and Omega (Christ)
altar
amillenarian
amillennialism
amillennialist
Amish
Anabaptist(s)
Ancient of Days, the (God)

angel
angel Gabriel, the
angel Jibril (Islamic version of Gabriel)
angel of the Lord
Angel of the Lord (if used as a theophany)
Anglo-Catholicism
Anglo-Saxon Church
Anima Christi (Latin for *Soul of Christ*)
annihilationism
Anno Domini
annunciation, the
Anointed One, the (Jesus Christ)
Anointed, the
anointing of the sick
ante-Christian
Ante Christum (BC; Latin for *Before Christ*)
ante-Nicene fathers
antiabortion, antiabortionist
antibiblical
Antichrist, the
anti-Christian
antinomian(s)
anti-Semitic, anti-Semite, anti-Semitism
anti-Trinitarian
Aphrodite
Apocalypse, the (Revelation)
apocalyptic literature
Apocrypha, the
apocryphal (adjective)
Apollonarianism

Apollonian
apologetics
apostasy, apostasies
apostate, apostatize
apostle
apostle Peter, Peter the apostle
Apostle to the Gentiles (Paul)
apostles
Apostles' Creed
apostolic age
apostolic benediction
apostolic council
apostolic faith
apostolic succession
Aramaic
archangel
archdeacon, archdeaconry
archdiocese
archenemy
archrival
Arian, Arianism
ark, the (Noah's)
ark narratives, the
ark of testimony
ark of the covenant
Armageddon
Arminian, Arminianism
Articles of Religion, the
    (Methodism)
AS (Anno Salutis, in the year of
    salvation)
Ascension Day
ascension of Christ, the
Ascension, the

ascetic, asceticism
Ash Wednesday
Ashkenazi Jew
Association of Research and
    Enlightenment (movement,
    also known as A.R.E.)
Assyrian Empire, the
astrology
Athanasian Creed
atheism
Atonement, the
atonement of Christ, the
Augsburg Confession
Authorized Version (or King
    James Version)
avatar
ayatollah (but Ayatollah
    Khomeni)
B'nai B'rith
Baals of Canaan
babe (of Bethlehem)
baby Jesus, the
Babylonian captivity
Babylonian exile
Baha'i (movement), Bahaism,
    Bahaist
Balaam
banshee
baptism, baptismal, baptize
baptism of the Holy Spirit
Baptism, the (of Christ); but
    Christ's baptism
baptistery (or baptistry)
baptistic

bar mitzvah
barbarian
Barmen Declaration
Basel, Confession of
bat (or bas or bath) mitzvah
Battle of Armageddon
BC (400 BC, but AD 70)
BCE (Before the Common Era)
Beast, the (Antichrist)
Beatific Vision
Beatitudes, the (Sermon on the
    Mount)
Beelzebub
Beghards
Being (God)
believers church
Beloved Apostle, the
Benedictines
benediction
beneficence
benison
Bereans
Beth Shan
betrayal, the (of Christ)
Bhagavad Gita (or
    Bhagavadgita)
Bible Belt
Bible school
Bible, the
Bible conference (but Niagara
    Bible Conference)
biblical
blasphemy
blessed name (Christ)

Blessing of Jacob
blood of Christ
bodhisattva (or boddhisattva)
body of Christ (the church)
book of Genesis, the (et al.)
Book of Life
book of the annals of Solomon,
    the
book of the annals of the kings
    of Israel (Judah et al.), the
Book of the Covenant
Book of the Dead
Book of the Law
Book of the Twelve, the
Book of Truth
Book, the (Bible)
born-again (adjective)
boy Jesus, the
brazen altar
Bread of Life (Bible or Christ)
Breeches Bible
bride of Christ (the church)
bridegroom, the (Christ)
brotherhood of man
Buddha, Buddhism, Buddhist
burnt offering
Byzantine
Cabala, Cabbalah (or Kabala)
Calvary
Calvinism
Canaan, Canaanite(s)
Canon, the (Scripture)
canon law
canon of Scripture, the

canonical
Captivity, the
catholic (universal)
Catholic Church (Roman
    Catholic)
Catholic Epistles (James et al.)
Catholicism
cause (of Christ)
CE (Common Era)
celestial city
century, first, nineteenth et al.
Chalcedon, Council of
Chanukah or Hanukkah (Feast of
    the Dedication)
charisma
charismatic
charismatic Christian
charismatic church
charismatic movement, the
charismatics
cherub, cherubim
chief priest
Chief Shepherd (Christ)
child of God (Christian)
Children of God, the (movement,
    also known as the Family of
    Love)
children of Israel
chosen people, the (Jews)
Christ
Christ child
Christ event
Christadelphians, the
christen, christened, christening
Christendom

Christian
Christian Brothers
Christian era
Christian Reformed Church
Christian Science (movement)
Christianize, Christianization
Christianlike
Christlike
Christmas Day
Christmas Eve
Christmastide
Christological
Christology
Christus Victor
Chronicler, the
church (body of Christ, universal)
church (building, service, local)
church age
church and state
church fathers
church invisible
church militant
Church of England
Church of Rome
church-planting (adj.)
church triumphant
church universal
church visible
church year, the (calendar)
City of David
City of the Lord (Jerusalem)
Cloud of Unknowing (classic
    mystical book)
codex (but Codex Sinaiticus)
collect (written prayer)

Comforter, the (Holy Spirit)
commandment (first, tenth,
   et al.)
commandment (generic term)
(Ten) Commandments, the
Communion (Lord's Supper)
Communion of Saints
Communion service
Complutensian Polyglot Bible
Concord, Book of
Concord, Formula of
Confessing Church
confession
Confession of Augsburg
confirmation
Confucian, Confucianism,
   Confucianist
Confucius
Congregationalists
consecration
Conservative Baptist
conservative, conservatism
consubstantiation
Corpus Christi (Latin for *body of*
   Christ)
Council of Nicea, Council of
   Trent, etc.
Counselor, the
covenant of grace
covenant of works
covenant theologian
Covenant Theology
covenant, the
covet
Creation, the

creation of man, the
Creationism
Creator, the
creed (but Nicene Creed, etc.)
cross (the object)
cross, the (event, not object)
Crucifixion, the
crucifixion of Christ
Crusades, the
cryptogram
cult
curate
curse, the
Daniel's Seventieth Week
Davidic covenant
Davidic dynasty
Davidic law
David's court
Day (capitalize when part of
    name of holiday or day
    marked by special observance)
Day of Atonement (Yom Kippur)
day of grace
Day of Judgment
Day of Pentecost
Day of the Lord
deacon (but Deacon Smith)
Dead Sea Scrolls
Decalogue, the
decree of Cyrus
deism, deist(s)
deity of Christ
Deity, the (God)
deluge, the (the flood)
Demiurge (God)

demon, demonic, demonolatry,
    demonology
determinism
deus ex machina
Deuteronomic
devil
Devil, the (Satan)
dharma
Diaspora, the (dispersion of Israel)
Didache
disciple(s)
Disciples of Christ
Dispensation of the Law
dispensationalism,
    dispensationalist
Dispersion, the
Dissenters (specific religious
    movement)
divine
Divine Father
divine guidance
divine judgment
Divine Providence
divinity of Christ, the
Divinity, the (God)
Docetism
Doctors of the Church (title for
    Ambrose, Augustine of
    Hippo, Gregory the Great,
    and Jerome)
doctrinal, doctrine
Documentary Hypothesis
dogma, dogmatic
Donatism
Door, the (Christ)

Douay (Rheims-Douay) Version
double predestination
Downgrade Controversy
doxology (but Gloria Patri)
Dragon, the (Satan)
dualism
early church
earth (dirt or ground, or when
    meaning *world*)
Earth (planet)
Easter morning
Easter Sunday
Eastern church
Eastern Orthodox Church
Eastern religions
Eastern rites
Ebionitism
ecclesia (or ekklesia)
ecclesiology
Eckankar (movement)
ecumenical movement
ecumenism, ecumenical
efficacious grace
Egnatian Way (Via Egnatia)
El
El Shaddai
election
Eleven, the
Elohim
Emmaus road
end times, the
Enemy, the (Satan)
England, Church of
Enlightenment, the
Epiphany

episcopacy, episcopal (relating to church government)
Episcopalian (denomination)
epistemological, epistemology
epistle (John's epistle et al.)
Epistle to the Romans et al.
Epistles, the (apostolic letters)
eschatology, eschatological
eschaton, the
Essene(s)
est (movement, stands for Erhard Seminars Training)
Eternal, the (God)
Eternal God
eternal life
eternity
Eucharist, the
Evangel, the
evangelical (adj., but First Evangelical Sunday School)
evangelical(s) (noun)
Evangelicalism (the movement)
Evangelist (Gospel writer)
evangelist (one who evangelizes)
Evil One, the (Satan)
ex cathedra
ex officio
Executor of justice, the (God)
exegesis
Exile, the
exodus from Egypt, the
Exodus, the
exorcism
expiation
extrabiblical

extreme unction
faith, the (Christian)
faith healing
fakir
Fall, the
fall of man
False Prophet (of Revelation)
Family of Love, the (movement, also known as the Children of God)
Father (God)
Father of Lies (Satan)
fatherhood of God
Fathers, the (but church fathers)
fatweh
feast
Feast of the Passover (Booths, Dedication, Esther, Firstfruits, Lights, Purim, Tabernacles, Unleavened Bread)
first Adam
First Advent, the
First Vatican Council, etc.
Firstborn, the (Christ)
Five Pillars of Faith (Islam)
Five Points of Calvinism
Flood, the
Formal Cause
four gospels, the (but the Gospels, when using as a title)
Four Kingdoms, the
Foursquare Gospel, International Church of the
Franciscans
free will (n), freewill (adj.)

Free Will Baptist
Freemason(s), Freemasonry
Friend (when meaning God, Christ, or the Holy Spirit)
fundamentalists (but Fundamentalism when referring to the movement)
fundamentals of the faith
futurist(s)
Galilean, the (Christ)
Galilee, Sea of (but Galilean sea)
Garden of Eden
garden, the
gatekeeper
gehenna
General Epistles
gentile (adj.)
Gentile(s)
Geschichte (German for *history*)
Gethsemane, Garden of
Gezer
Gloria Patri (but the doxology)
glory cloud
glossolalia
gnostic (generic or descriptive)
Gnosticism (specific form of)
God
god (pagan)
God of gods and Lord of lords
God's house
God's Word (Bible)
God's word (promise)
Godhead (essential being of God)
godhead (godship or godhood)

godless
godlike
godly
God-man
godsend
Godspeed
Golden Rule, the
golden text
Golgotha
Good Book, the
Good Friday
Good News, the (i.e., the Gospel)
Good Samaritan, the
Good Shepherd (Jesus)
good shepherd, the parable of the
gospel (adj.)
gospel (John's gospel et al.)
gospel, the (specific New Testament concept of the good news or God's redemption)
Gospel(s), the
grace
Great Awakening
Great Commandment
Great Commission
Great High Priest (Christ)
Great Judgment
Great King
Great Physician
Great Schism
Great Shepherd
Great Tribulation
Great White Throne

Grecian
Greek
Guide, the (Holy Spirit)
hades (hell)
Hades (mythological)
Hagiographa
hagiographer, hagiographic,
    hagiography
Hail Mary
Hallel
hallelujah
Hannah's song
Hanukkah or Chanukah (Feast of
    the Dedication)
Hare Krishnas, the (movement,
    also known as the
    International Society of
    Krishna Consciousness)
Head, the (Christ, head of the
    church)
heaven
heavenly Father
Hebraic
Hebrew
Hebrew Bible
Hebrew patriarchs
Hegira (Muhammad's)
Heidelberg Catechism
Heilsgeschichte (German for
    salvation history)
hell
Hellenism, Hellenistic
Helvetic Confessions
hermeneutics
Herod's temple

Herodian
heterodoxy
High Church (Anglican)
high priest, a
High Priest, the (Christ)
High Priestly Prayer, the (Christ's)
higher criticism
Hillel
Historical Books, the (part of the
    Old Testament)
historical-grammatical
    hermeneutics
historicist(s)
Holiness Movement, the
holocaust (when referring to a
    general destruction or sacri-
    fice or fire, etc.)
Holocaust (when referring to the
    specific event during World
    War II)
Holy Bible
Holy Book (Bible)
Holy City (Jerusalem)
Holy Club, the (Oxford)
Holy Communion
Holy Eucharist
holy family
Holy Ghost
Holy Grail
Holy Land (Palestine)
Holy of Holies
holy oil
Holy One, the (God, Christ)
Holy One of Israel, the (God)
holy orders

holy place
Holy Roller
Holy Saturday
Holy Scriptures
Holy Spirit
Holy Thursday
Holy Trinity
holy water
Holy Week (before Easter)
Holy Writ (Bible)
Holy Year (Catholic)
homeland
homiletics, homilies, homily
house of David
house of the Lord
Huguenots
Humanae Vitae (Latin for *human lives*)
Hussites
Hutterites
hymnal
hymnbook
hypostatic union
ichthus
icon
idealist(s)
idolatry
illuminati
imago dei (Latin for *image of God*)
Immaculate Conception, the
Immanuel
immortality of the soul
in excelsis
incarnation of Christ, the

Incarnation, the
inerrancy, inerrant
infallibility
inner veil
Inquisition, the
inspiration
intercession
Intercessor, the (Christ)
intertestamental
intifada
invisible church
Isaian (or Isaianic)
Islamic Jihad (the organization, but jihad, in a general sense)
Jacob's Trouble
Jacobites
Jebusites
Jehovah
Jehovah's Witnesses (officially, the Watchtower Bible and Tract Society)
Jeremian (or Jeremianic)
Jerome
Jerusalem
Jesuits (Society of Jesus, but jesuitical)
Jesus Christ
Jesus Prayer, the
Jew(s)
Jewish (adj.)
Jewish Feast (Passover)
Jewish New Year (Rosh Hashanah/Hoshanah)
Jewish Talmud

Jew's (Jews') harp
jihad (but Islamic Jihad, when
    referring to a specific organi-
    zation)
Johannine
John the Baptist
John the Evangelist
Jordan River (but the river
    Jordan)
Jordan Valley
Josephus
Jubilee (year of emancipation)
Judah, Judahite
Judaic, Judaica
Judaism, Judaist, Judaistic
Judaize(r)
Judea
Judean
Judeo-Christian
Judge (the Lord)
judges, the
Judgment Day
judgment seat of Christ, the
Judgment, Great White Throne
Judgment, the Last
justification
Kaddish (special prayer)
kenosis, kenosistic
kerygma
Keswick Convention
kibbutz, kibbutzim
king
King (God or Jesus)
King David, King Herod, etc.

King James Version
King of Glory (Christ)
King of kings
King of kings (God the only
    Ruler)
King of the Jews
Kingdom, the (God's)
kingdom age
kingdom of God
kingdom of heaven
kingdom of Israel
kingdom of Satan
Kings (books of 1 and 2 Kings as
    single literary work)
kingship of Christ
Kinsman-Redeemer
Knesset (Israel's governing body)
koine
koinonia
Koran (but prefer Qur'an)
koranic
Lady Folly
Lady Wisdom
laity
lake of fire
Lamb, the (Christ)
Lamb of God
Lamb's Book of Life
land of Canaan
land of Goshen
Land of Promise
Last Day, the
last days, the
Last Judgment, the

last rites (extreme unction)
Last Supper, the
Late Bronze Age (1550–1200 BC)
Latin Rite
Latin Vulgate
Latter Rain movement
law (as opposed to grace)
Law, the (Pentetuch)
law and the prophets, the
law of Moses, a (general)
Law of Moses, the
Lawgiver (God)
layperson
Lent, Lenten
Leviathan
Levites, Levitical
liberal, liberalism
Liberation Theology
Light (Christ)
limbo (Roman Catholic
   theological term)
Litany, the (Anglican), but litany
   in a general sense
liturgy
living God
living Word, the (Bible)
Logos, the (Jesus)
Lord of hope (of love, of faith-
   fulness, of salvation, etc.)
Lord of Hosts
Lord of Lords
Lord, the
Lord's Anointed, the (Christ)
Lord's Day, the
Lord's Prayer, the (or the Our

Father)
Lord's Supper, the
Lord's Table, the
lordship of Christ, the
Lost Tribes, the (BUT lost tribes
   of Israel)
Love Chapter, the
Low Church (Anglican)
Lucan (or Lukan)
Lucifer
Luther's Ninety-five Theses
Lutheran, Lutheranism
Maccabees
Magi
Magisterium
Magnificat, the
Mahabharata
major prophets (people)
Major Prophets, the (Old
   Testament)
Majority Text
Maker (God)
mammon
Man of Sin
Man of Sorrows
Maranatha
Marcan (or Markan)
Marcionism
martyrdom
Masoretic text
mass (service)
Mass, the (sacrament)
Master (the one supreme God)
Master, the (Christ)
Matthean

matzo ball
Maundy Thursday (Holy
    Thursday)
mazel tov
Mediator, the (Christ)
medieval
Mediterranean
megachurch
Megiddo
Mennonites
menorah
mercy seat
Mesopotamia, Mesopotamian
Messiah, the (Christ)
messianic
Messianic King
Methodist, Methodism
Middle East, Middle Eastern
midrash
midtribulation, midtribulational,
    midtribulationism, midtribu-
    lationist
millenarian, millenarianism,
    millenarianist
millennial kingdom (note the -ll
    and -nn spellings)
millennialist, millennialism
millennium, millenniums,
    millennia (1,000 years)
Millennium, the
mini-narratives
minor prophets (people)
Minor Prophets (the books)
Miserere, the
Mishnah

misseo Dei
Moabite Stone, the
modernism
monarchy, the
Monophysite, Monophysitism
Montanism
Mormon, Mormonism (officially,
    the Church of Jesus Christ of
    Latter-Day Saints)
Mosaic
Mosaic Code (Pentateuch or Ten
    Commandments)
Mosaic Law (Pentateuch or Ten
    Commandments)
Most High God, the
Mount of Olives
Mount of Transfiguration, the
Mount Olivet Discourse (but
    Olivet discourse)
Mount Sinai
muezzin
mufti
Muhammad (preferred over
    Mohammad)
mullah
Muratorian Canon
Muslim (preferred over Moslem)
mystery
name of Christ, the
nativity of Christ, the
Nativity, the (the celebration)
Near East, Near Eastern
neoorthodox, neoorthodoxy
neo-Pentecostalism
neoplatonic, neoplatonism

New Age movement, the
new birth
New Covenant, the
    (New Testament)
new heaven and new earth
new Israel
New Jerusalem
New Testament church
New Thought (movement)
Nicene Creed
Nicene fathers
nonbiblical
non-Christian (n. and adj., but
    unchristian)
Nonconformists (religious
    movement)
nonliteral
North Galatian theory, the
northern kingdom (Israel)
NT
Nunc Dimittis
obeisance
occult, the
Old Covenant, the (Old
    Testament)
Olivet discourse (but Mount
    Olivet Discourse)
Omega, the
Omnipotent, the
One, the
one true God, the
Only Begotten, the
only begotten of the Father
only begotten Son of God
oracle (of doom, hope, etc.)

ordain, ordained, ordination
Order of Ministers
Order of Preachers (but the order,
    the Dominican order, etc.)
original sin
orthodox, orthodoxy
Orthodox Church, the
OT
Our Father, the (or the Lord's
    Prayer)
Oxford Group, the (movement,
    also known as Moral Re-
    Armament)
Oxford Movement
Palestine, Palestinian
Palestine covenant
Palm Sunday
papacy
papal infallibility
papyrus
parable of the prodigal son, the
Paraclete, the
paradise (Garden of Eden)
paradise (heaven)
Parousia, the
Paschal Lamb (Jesus)
Passion, the
Passion of Christ, the
Passion Sunday
Passion Week
Passover Feast, Seder
Passover Lamb (Jesus)
Passover, the
pastor, pastoral
Pastoral Epistles

Pastoral Letters
Paternoster (the Lord's Prayer)
patriarch, a
Patriarch, the (Abraham)
patriarchs, the (Hebrew)
patriarch, patriarchies
Patripassionism
patristic(s)
Paul, the apostle et al.
Paul's epistles
Paul's letters
Pauline Epistles
Peace, The (or The Kiss of Peace)
Pelagianism
penal substitution
penitence
Pentateuch, Pentateuchal
Pentecost
Pentecostal, Pentecostalism
people of God, the
Persia, Persian
person of Christ, the
Pesach (Passover)
Peshitta
Petrine
Pharaoh (without article, as a
    title)
pharaoh, the (general)
pharisaic (attitude)
Pharisaic (pertaining to the
    Pharisees)
Pharisee(s)
Pietism
piety, pietist(s), pietistic
Pilgrims, the

pillar of cloud
pillar of fire
plains of Moab
PLO (Palestinian Liberation
    Organization)
Poetic Books, the
polytheism
pontiff, the
pope, the
Pope John Paul II et al.
postbiblical
post-Christian
postexilic
postmillennial, postmillennial-
    ism, postmillennialist
post-Nicene fathers
posttribulation, posttribula-
    tional, posttribulationism,
    posttribulationist
pre-Christian
predestination
preexilic
premillenarian, premillenarian-
    ism
premillennial, premillennialism,
    premillennialist
premils
Presbyterian, Presbyterianism,
    Presbytery of Greater Atlanta
    et al.
presbytery (in a general sense)
Presence (God, Christ, or Holy
    Spirit)
presence (when used otherwise)
preterist(s)

pretribulation, pretribulational,
    pretribulationism, pretribula-
    tionist
priesthood of believers
priesthood of Christ
Prime Mover
Prince of Darkness
Prince of Peace
Prison Epistles
Prison Letters
proabortion, but pro-abortionist
pro-choice
Prodigal Son, the
pro-life
Promised Land, the
Promised One, the
promise-doctrine
promise-plan
proof-texts
prophet Isaiah (etc.), the
Prophet of Doom, the (Jeremiah,
    but Jeremiah was a prophet
    of doom)
Prophetic Books, the
Prophets, the (books of Old
    Testament)
prophets, the (people)
Protestant, Protestantism
Providence (as a name for God)
providence of God
Psalm 41, etc.
psalm, a
psalmist, the
Psalms, the (Old Testament)
psalter, a

Psalter, the (the Psalms)
pseudepigrapha, pseude-
    pigraphal
purgatory
Purim (Feast of Esther)
Puritan(s), Puritanism
pyx
Q (for *Quelle*)
Qoheleth (Hebrew for *the
    teacher of wisdom*)
Quakers (also known as the
    Society of Friends)
queen (but Queen of Sheba, etc.)
Quelle (German for *source*)
quietism
Qumran
Qumran Essenes
quo vadis? (Latin for *where are
    you going?*)
Qur'an (preferred, but also
    Qu'ran, Quran, Koran)
rabbi
rabbinic, rabbinical
Rahab
Ramadan
Ranters
Rapture, the (specific event)
rapture, the (doctrine of)
rapture of Christ (or the church)
Rastafarian, Rastafarianism
Real Presence (of Christ)
Received Text, the
reconciliation
Redeemer (Christ)
Redeemer-King

Reformation (Protestant)
reformation movement
Reformed Church in America
Reformed church(es)
Reformed theology
Reformers, the (specific group)
reincarnation
religion
Religious Right, the
remnant, the
Renaissance, the
Restoration, the (under Cyrus)
restoration movement
Resurrection, the
resurrection of Christ, the
resurrection of the body (of the
    dead, etc.)
revelation
Revelation (NT book)
Reverend (Smith, etc.)
reverend, reverence
righteous, righteousness
Rig-Veda
rite(s)
ritual
river (but capitalize when part
    of proper name: Jordan
    River)
Rock, the (Christ)
Roman Catholic Church
Roman Catholicism
Roman church
Roman Empire
Roman Rite
rosary, the

Rosh Hashanah, Hoshanah
    (Jewish New Year)
Rosicrucianism (movement)
Rule of Faith (Bible)
Ruler (God)
Sabbatarian, Sabbatarianism
sabbath (age)
Sabbath (day)
sabbatical (n. and adj.)
Sabellianism
sacerdotalism
sacrament(s)
sacramentalism, sacramentalist
Sacramentarian(ism)
Sacred Host
sacred rite(s)
sacrilege, sacrilegious
Sadducee(s)
Saint Peter et al.
saints, the
Salat al-fajr (special prayer)
Salvation Army
salvation history
salvific (adj.)
Samaria
Samaritan
sanctus
Sanhedrin
Satan
satanic, satanist, satanism
Savior
sayings of the wise
schism
Scholasticism
Scientology (movement)

scriptural
Scripture(s) (Bible, n. and adj.)
scripture(s) (other religions)
sea (capitalize when part of
    proper name: Red Sea, Sea of
    Galilee, etc.)
Second Adam, the (Christ)
Second Advent, the
Second Blessing, the
Second Coming, the
second coming of Christ, the
Second Great Awakening, the
second Joshua, the (Jesus)
Second Person of the Trinity
seder
Seekers, the
Selah (Hebrew liturgical notation)
Semi-Pelagianism
Semite, Semitic, Semitism
sensus plenior
Sephardic Jew
Sepuagesima
Septuagint (LXX)
seraph, seraphim
Sermon on the Mount
Serpent, the (Satan)
Seven Deadly Sins (pride, cov-
    etousness, lust, envy, glut-
    tony, anger, and sloth)
seven sacraments, the
Seventh-day Adventist,
    Seventh-day Adventism
Seventieth Week
Shabbat
Shabuoth (Pentecost)

Shakers, the
shalom
shalom aleichem
Shechina or Shekinh
Shema, the
Sheol
Shepherd Psalm, the
Shiite/Shi'ite
Shiloh
Shrove Tuesday
Shulammite
sign of the cross
sin offering
Sinai covenant, the
Sin-Bearer, the
Social Gospel
Society of Jesus (Jesuits)
Sola Fide
Sola Gratia
Sola Scriptura
Solomonic
Solomon's temple
son of David (Jesus)
Son of God (Jesus)
son of man (Ezekiel)
Son of Man (Jesus)
Song of Moses
Song of Songs (Solomon's)
sons of God (Christians)
sonship of Christ
soteriology
South Galatian theory, the
southern kingdom (Judah)
sovereign God
sovereign Lord

Spirit (when meaning the Holy
Spirit; otherwise lowercase)
spirit of the age, the
spirit-guides
Star of David, the
stations of the cross
Stoicism (but *stoic* when used in
a general sense)
Strangites, the
Sublapsarian
Subordinationism,
Subordinationist
Suffering Servant
Sufi, Sufism
Sukkoth (Feast of Booths)
Sunday school (unless referring
to a particular Sunday school,
as in Walker Memorial
Sunday School)
Sunna
Supralapsarian, Supralapsarianism
Supreme Being, the
sutra
Swedenborgianism (movement,
also known as the Church of
the New Jerusalem)
synagogue
syncretism
synod (but Synod of Middle
Tennessee, etc.)
Synoptic Gospels
Synoptic Problem, the
synoptics, the
Syriac
systematic theology

tabernacle, the (building)
table (the Lord's, etc.)
table of shewbread
Taliban, the
Talmud
Talmudic
Tanach
Tao, the (first principle of uni-
verse)
Taoism (Chinese philosophy)
Targum
targumic
Te Deum Laudamus (Latin for
We praise you, O God)
Teacher, the (*qoheleth*)
Teacher of Righteousness, the
Teacher of wisdom, the
(*Qoheleth*)
tehillim (Hebrew for *praises*)
Temple, Solomonic
temple, the (at Jerusalem)
Temple Mount, the Mount
temple of the Lord, the
Temptation, the (Christ's)
temptation in the desert, the
temptation of Christ, the
Ten Articles, the (Anglican)
Ten Commandments (but the
fifth commandment)
Ten Tribes, the
ten tribes of Israel, the
Tent of Meeting
Tent of the Testimony
tephillot (Hebrew for *prayers*)
Testaments, the

Tetragrammaton, the (YHWH)
Textus Receptus
theodicy
theology
theophany
Theophilus
Theosophical Society
Theosophy, theosophist
Thirty Years' War
Thirty-nine Articles, the
(Anglican)
Thomist, Thomism
three persons of the Trinity, the
throne of grace, the
Thummim
Time of Jacob's Trouble, the
Time of the Gentiles, the
time of the judges, the
Torah
Tower of Babel
Transcendental Meditation (move-
ment, also known as TM)
Transfiguration, the
transubstantiation
Trappists
Tree of Knowledge (of Good and
Evil)
Tree of Life
tribe of Judah
Tribulation, the Great
Trinitarian, Trinitarianism
Trinity, the (but doctrine of the
trinity)
Tripitaka
Triumphal Entry, the

triune God
Truth (the gospel, God's truth,
ultimate truth)
Twelve, the (disciples)
twelve apostles, the
Twelve Articles, the
twelve prophets, the (minor
prophets)
Twenty-third Psalm
Ugarit (kingdom of)
Ultramontanism
unchristian (but non-Christian)
un-Christlike
unction of the sick
underground church
ungodly
Unification Church, the
(movement)
Unitarians (the Unitarian
Universalist Association)
united kingdom (of Israel)
Unity School of Christianity, the
(movement)
universal church
universalism
unlimited atonement
unscriptural
Upanishads
Upper Room, the
Upper Room Discourse
Urim
Vatican Council, First (Second)
Vedas, Vedic
Veneration of the Cross
Veneration of the Saints

venial sin
vestments
vestry
Via Dolorosa (Latin for *the sorrowful way*)
Via Egnatia (Egnatian Way)
viaticum; plural viaticums or viatica
Vicar of Christ (pope)
visible church
vocation
Voice, the (Holy Spirit)
Vulgate
Wailing Wall (Western Wall)
Waldenses, Waldensians
Water of Life (Christ)
Way, the (Christ)
Way International, the (movement)
(the) way, the truth, and the life
weltanschauung (German for *worldview*)
Wesleyanism
Western church
Western Rites
Western thought, etc.
Western Wall (Wailing Wall)
Westminster Catechism
Westminster Confession
Westminster Standards
Whitsunday (preferred, but also Whit Sunday)
Wicca
Wicked One, the (Satan)
will of God
Vicar of Peter (pope)
Vicar, vicarage
Victor, the (Christ)
vigil
Vine, the (Christ)
Vinegar Bible
virgin birth, the
Virgin Mary, the
Vishnu
Wisdom Literature, the
wise men (kings of the Orient who visited the Christ child)
Witness of the Spirit
Word, the (Bible or Christ)
Word made flesh (Christ)
Word of God (Bible)
Word of God (Christ)
Word of Life
Word of Truth
Work of Christ (salvation)
worldview
worshiped, worshiping, worshiper (preferable) OR worshipped, worshipping, worshipper
Writings, the
Yahrzeit
Yahweh, Yahwehwism, Yahwehwist, Yahwehwistic (or YHWH or YHVH)
yarmulke
Year of Jubilee
YHWH (or YHVH)
Yoga (Hindu system)
Yom Kippur (Day of Atonement)

Footnotes and References for General Audiences (16.1–.120)

A. General Rules

It is the author's responsibility to provide complete and accurate footnotes as part of the manuscript prior to its undergoing the editorial process.

1. Number footnotes consecutively throughout each chapter of the book, beginning with the number 1 in each new chapter.

2. Type the footnotes on sheets separate from the text. Double-space them with generous margins.

3. In published form, notes are usually printed at the end of the book, not at the end of each chapter or at page bottoms. The publisher will make the decision about the appropriate place to put them. In the disk/printout given to the publisher, the notes should appear at chapter ends or at the end of the book—not in a footnote window.

4. Each footnote for a book should include the following information:

> Author's full name
> Complete title of book

Editor, compiler, or translator, if any

Edition, if other than the first

Number of volumes

Facts of publication—city where published, publisher, date of publication

Volume number (if any)

Page number(s) of the particular citation (Omit the abbreviations *p.* or *pp.* from the citations.)

5. When citing an article from a periodical as the source, the following information should appear:

Author's full name

Title of the article

Name of the periodical

Volume (and number) of the periodical

Date of the volume or issue

Page number(s) of the particular citation (Again, omit the abbreviations *p.* or *pp.* in the citations.)

6. After the first reference to a particular work in each chapter, subsequent references in the same chapter should be in shortened formats. The shortened reference should include only the last name of the author and the short title of the book in italics or of the magazine/ journal article enclosed in quotation marks, followed by the page numbers of the reference.

1. Harold G. Henderson, *An Introduction to Haiku: An Anthology of Poems and Poets from Basho to Shiki* (New York: Doubleday Anchor Books, 1958), 124.

2. A. L. Clauson, "Religious Imagery in Dylan's Later Songs," *Poetry and Christianity* 15 (Summer 2001), 110.

3 Fyodor Dostoevsky, *The Possessed* (New York: Signet Classics, 1962), 224.

4. Henderson, *An Introduction to Haiku,* 78.

5. Clauson, "Religious Imagery in Dylan's Later Songs," 112.

7. *Ibid.* is acceptable for referring to a single work cited in the note immediately preceding. It takes the place of the author's name, the title of the work, and the succeeding identical material. Incidentally, use Roman type for Latin words and abbreviations in footnotes: Ibid., et al., op cit., inter alia, idem.

11. C. S. Lewis, *The Allegory of Love: A Study in Medieval Tradition* (Oxford: Clarendon Press, 1936), 259.

12. Ibid., 360.

B. Internet References
(17.180–, .187, 17.234–37)

Citing from the Internet is a relatively new area in scholarship. We suggest caution in quoting from Web-based sources, as it is difficult to verify the level of expertise or credentials behind some of the information available online. Follow the general rules for citing sources in books or periodicals, attempting to be as complete as possible. Following are some examples:

1. C. E. Ediger, "You Can't Kid a Quilter," from "Quilting Graffiti," *Quilters Anonymous* online magazine, from *Quilting Monthly* (2 December 2001), quiltingmonthly.com/anonymous/graffiti.

2. Ken Stephens and David Shepherd, "A Brief History of Nashville Publishing," About.com, 20 April 2000 (accessed June 20, 2001).

3. Shawn L. Stanford, "A Meeting of the Minds: Creation of the Arizona Constitution," Web-based article taken from the Introduction to *Liberty and*

Justice: The Writing of the Arizona State Constitution (Phoenix: Published for the Arizona Constitutional Preservation Administration by the State of Arizona Archives Trust Fund Board, Arizona Archives and Records Foundation, 1998), http:www.azconst.gov.

C. Scripture References (8.111–.115, 17.246–.249)

1. It is the author's responsibility to provide accurate and complete references to the Bible.

2. Do not abbreviate books of the Bible when you cite a reference without specific chapter and verse.

> Deuteronomy is one of the first five books of the Bible commonly known as the Pentateuch.

3. In a citation in block quotations, it is proper form to abbreviate the names of Bible books. (See pages 228-229, Section D, "Abbreviations and Scripture References.")

4. Use Arabic numerals to cite all references to Scripture.

> 1 Chronicles   2 Peter   3 John

5. It is acceptable to abbreviate the names of Bible versions when citing a reference. (See pages 229-230, Section D, "Abbreviations and Scripture References.")

6. When quoting Scripture, place the period after the parentheses containing the reference. If the quotation ends in a question or exclamation point, place it with the text and place a period after the last parenthesis.

> "Finally, my brothers, rejoice in the Lord" (Phil. 3:1).
>
> "'If I want him to remain until I come,' Jesus answered, 'what is that to you?'" (John 21:21)

Biographical Sketches

Leonard G. Goss is senior acquisitions editor at Broadman & Holman Publishers, the book publishing division of LifeWay Christian Resources. Before taking this position, he led editorial efforts at Crossway Books, Zondervan Publishing House, and the Evangelical Book Club. He began his publishing career with John Wiley & Sons. Len has solicited, developed, and edited more than a thousand books and has launched many writing careers in both the fiction and nonfiction fields. He is the coauthor, with Don Aycock, of *Writing Religiously* and *The Christian Writer's Book,* and together they edited *Inside Religious Publishing.*

Len and his wife Carolyn live in Nashville, have two adult sons, and are the coauthors of *The Little Style Guide to Great Christian Writing and Publishing.* He enjoys walking, reading, occasionally playing golf (not successfully), playing guitar, and watching PAC-10 football. His dog Jack is better than other dogs.

Don M. Aycock is a pastor, writer, and conference leader. He has spent most of his career in pastoral ministry. He has written or edited more than twenty books, including *God's Man, Still God's Man,* coauthored with Mark Sutton, *Prayer 101, Eight Days That Changed the*

World, Living By the Fruit of the Spirit, and *How to Have a Conversation with God.* Don is married to Carla, and they have twin sons who are grown. He speaks at writers' conferences around the country and also leads seminars for men's groups. He has a doctorate in theology. In his leisure time Don loves to haul in red snapper from the Gulf of Mexico and largemouth bass from anywhere. He also enjoys trying to figure out all those wonderful guitar licks from the late Chet Atkins (whom he once met). Don can be contacted through his Web site at www.donaycock.net.